M 5

Wh e
M

PUBLISHING

New York

Acknowledgments

This book was a collaborative effort on the part of Kaplan's MCAT team: Samantha Fallon, Owen Farcy, Adam Grey, Aaron Lemon-Strauss, Keith Lubeley, Alexander Macnow, Petros Minasi, Jr., and Deeangelee Pooran.

Special thanks to Mikhail Alexeeff, Erik Bowman, Kim Bowers, Dom Eggert, Tyler Fraser, Joanna Graham, Allison Harm, Maureen McMahon, Maria Nicholas, Neha Rao, Amjed Saffarini, Scott Safir, Thomas Sargent, Sylvia Tidwell Scheuring, Logan Stark, and Stephen Sylwestrak.

MCAT® is registered trademark of the Association of American Medical Colleges, which neither sponsors nor endorses this product.

Published by Kaplan Publishing, a division of Kaplan, Inc.
395 Hudson Street
New York, NY 10014

Printed in the United States of America

10 9 8 7 6 5 4 3

ISBN: 978-1-61865-358-1

Kaplan Publishing books are available at special quantity discounts to use for sales promotions, employee premiums, or educational purposes. For more information or to purchase books, please call the Simon & Schuster special sales department at 866-506-1949.

TABLE OF CONTENTS

Introduction

And now it starts: your long, yet fruitful journey toward wearing a white coat. Proudly wearing that white coat, though, is only part of your motivation. You are reading this book because you want to be a healer.

Studying for any test isn't fun, but it doesn't have to be a nightmare, either.

Studying for a test that is still undergoing its final development, however, is even more of a challenge.

We are at a unique point in the history of the MCAT. For the first time in over twenty years, the MCAT is undergoing a major and foundational change. Sure, the current version of the MCAT has evolved from an eight-hour-long, paper-and-pencil exam to a three-and-a-half-hour computer-based test, but we now stand at the crossroads of a revolution in this exam which coincides with a defining moment in medicine and healthcare. Healthcare is changing. Medicine is changing. The skills that are valued in a physician are changing. And the change in the MCAT reflects a transformation in what is expected of incoming medical students.

In this book, we have offered an interpretation for you, the student, into what this revolution of the MCAT means for you, your education, and your future. We will start out with an overview of the context of this change, and then dive into the specifics of what you need to know. Then, you will learn how to approach this new exam through examples and strategies, culminating in the experience of a practice version of the new MCAT along with thoughts on what you need to consider as you move forward with your preparation.

Here, we share with you what we know about the new MCAT as it stands now, but you can expect that we will keep you informed as we continue to learn more about the changes to the exam.

On behalf of everyone at Kaplan, congratulations on taking these first steps toward your own white coat, and welcome to the beginning of your study of medicine.

Why Was the MCAT Created? (And What's It All About?)

We stand now at the beginning of a new era in medical education. As citizens of this 21st-century world of healthcare, we are charged with creating a patient-oriented, culturally competent, cost-conscious, universally available, technically advanced and research-focused healthcare system, run by compassionate providers. Suffice it to say, this is no easy task. Problem-based learning, integrated curricula, and classes in interpersonal skills are some of the responses to this demand for an excellent workforce—a workforce of which you'll soon be a part.

Congratulations on taking your first step in the journey to (and through) medical school!

A BRIEF HISTORY OF MEDICAL EDUCATION AND THE MCAT

While our understanding of the human body (and, by extension, our ability to diagnose and treat disease) has increased exponentially over the last century, medical education is in a similar position now that it was one hundred years ago. Reeling from the atrocities of

World War I and the severe morbidity it caused, the United States found itself in the midst of a physician shortage. Further, the *Flexner Report*,[1] an oft-cited treatise published by Abraham Flexner in 1910, recommended significant changes to the education of premedical and medical students alike. Most notably, the *Flexner Report* paved the way for the standardization of premedical curricula (the "three sciences" of biology, chemistry, and physics) and urged medical schools to find a common and consistent route of evaluating prospective students. Flexner also reformed medical education once students were already accepted to medical school: he pushed for the standard four-year curriculum (two years preclinical or "laboratory" science, such as anatomy, biochemistry, physiology, and pathology/pathophysiology; and two years clinical experience). Prior to the *Flexner Report*, schools set their curricula with no regulation, and students were often accepted with few or no academic credentials.

In the wake of this study, and perhaps partially from changes instituted *because* of the *Flexner Report*, attrition rates (the number of students dropping out) at medical schools began to climb, and—by the middle of the 1920s—up to one-half of incoming students were gone before graduation day. This was haunting to the medical community, which found itself torn between needing *more* physicians and needing more *skilled* physicians. How could medicine create a robust system for evaluating incoming students to assure medical schools that they were accepting all-stars who would be able to complete the requirements of medical school? Enter the MCAT.

From the Moss Test to 1991

It was from this academic climate that psychologist-physician Fred A. Moss developed the test that bore his name, also known as the Scholastic Aptitude Test for Medical Students (SATMS). This first version of the MCAT was composed of six to eight sections, each of which tested a different skill; these included memory, scientific reasoning and knowledge, reading comprehension, and logic.

---

1 Flexner A. Medical Education in the United States and Canada: A Report to the Carnegie Foundation for the Advancement of Teaching (The Flexner Report). *The Carnegie Foundation for the Advancement of Teaching.* 1910.

Chapter 1
Why Was the MCAT Created? (And What's It All About?)

K

The adoption of the Moss Test/SATMS as an admission credential directly reflected the establishment and standardization of modern medical education.

As medical schools began to downplay the psychological testing aspects of the Moss Test/SATMS and focus more on content knowledge and critical thinking skills, the test continued to evolve. In 1946, a four-part exam called the Professional School Aptitude Test was developed, with sections for quantitative, verbal, scientific content and application, and a section termed "Understanding Modern Society" (later, "General Information"). This section tested civics, economics, history, and sociology, making it somewhat similar to the new Psychological, Social, and Biological Foundations of Behavior section of MCAT 2015—and it probably flowed from similar drives as the current test revision. With an expanding American landscape, ever-increasing in its diversity, the modern physician must understand the society in which he or she works.

CHAPTER LINK

See Chapter 3 for information on *why* the MCAT is changing in 2015. See Chapter 9 for information on what is covered in the new Psychological, Social, and Biological Foundations of Behavior section. See Chapter 12 for examples of questions from this new section.

More subtle changes occurred until the early 1990s. The Medical College Admission Test acquired its current name in 1948, "General Information" was dropped in 1977, and the scoring was adjusted from a scale of 200–800 to a scale of 1–15. Score reporting also changed, with individual scores from each science being provided, rather than one common score for all sciences.

The Current MCAT: 1992 to January 2015

The paradigm for MCAT questions changed dramatically in 1992, when passage-based questions became the predominant question type on the exam. This may have been, in part, a response to the accusation that the MCAT was a memorization-driven, content-heavy exam. While the skills that the Association of American Medical Colleges (AAMC) are looking for are more thoroughly discussed later in this chapter, the change to passage-based questions heralded a need for test takers to be able to absorb new information *while taking the exam* and be able to integrate that information with what outside knowledge they already had.

The test sections were again changed, leading to the well-known four sections of today's MCAT: Physical Sciences, Verbal Reasoning, Biological Sciences, and the Writing Sample (dropped in 2013). While the Quantitative section was formally dropped in this same MCAT revision, the skills it tested (arithmetic, algebra, basic geometry and trigonometry, formula manipulation, estimation, and basic probability and statistics) were distributed throughout the science sections.

In 2007, the MCAT followed a number of other standardized exams[2] in becoming a computer-based test. For many students, this was a welcome change: the exam became nearly three hours shorter, at 4 hours and 20 minutes of total testing time; further, many students preferred the ability to type their writing samples rather than having to hand-write them. After all, doctors aren't really known for their perfect penmanship!

Finally, this test revision marked a vast increase in the number of times the MCAT was offered per year. As a paper-and-pencil test, the MCAT was available only twice annually, in April and August. Students would fill giant lecture halls on their school's campus. In contrast, the MCAT was offered 28 times in the 2012 calendar year, including both morning and afternoon administrations; the AAMC's partnership with Prometric limited the number of students who can

---

2 The first major standardized exam to become computer-based was the National Council Licensure Exam (NCLEX), which made the switch as early as 1994. This is the certifying examination for nurses.

Chapter 1
Why Was the MCAT Created? (And What's It All About?)

take any one exam (the test centers are of limited size), but increased the safety and security of the exam.

The transition to MCAT 2015 could be felt by test takers as early as January 2013. This test is notably shorter: it's dropped the Writing Sample, which is an hour of testing time back (3 hours, 20 minutes total testing time). This change was mostly due to the fact that admissions committees deemed this section by far the least important when making admissions decisions and noted the difficulty of analyzing the Writing Sample score, which was given as a letter on a scale from J to T, with T being the highest, next to the numerical score of the multiple-choice section, which ranges from 3 to 45, with 45 being the highest.

The January 2013 administrations of the MCAT also marked the first time the AAMC had tested material for MCAT 2015 on students at large. Following the Biological Sciences section, students who did not void their scores could choose to participate in the Trial Section, a 45-minute, 32-question, unscored section featuring questions on the new material for MCAT 2015: biochemistry, psychology and sociology, and biologically-based chemistry, and physics. As a reward for "put[ting] forth a good-faith effort,"[3] test takers received a $30 Amazon.com gift card and feedback on their performance in the section compared to the others who also participated.

MCAT 2015: Spring 2015 to 2030(?)

In this new era in medical education, the AAMC revisited the MCAT to see how it could play a role in arming the next generation of physicians for our developing health system. In 2008, the AAMC created the MR5 committee, tasked with assessing the MCAT and recommending appropriate changes to increase the exam's relevance for students and admissions committees alike.

How and why the MCAT is changing in 2015 is covered extensively in the next two chapters, so we'll leave those details behind for now. But we do know that this exam is here to stay. In the standardized

---

3 Trial Section. AAMC.org.

testing world, it's considered good form to revisit and review an exam about every fifteen years; as the AAMC reports, **this new version of the exam is likely to remain until at least 2030.**

CHAPTER LINK

See Chapter 2 for information on *how* the MCAT is changing in 2015.
See Chapter 3 for information on *why* the MCAT is changing in 2015.

IMPORTANT POINT

MCAT 2015 is here to stay. This new version of the exam is likely to remain until at least 2030.

FIVE COMMON MISCONCEPTIONS ABOUT THE MCAT

The utility of the MCAT as a testing resource, its role in admissions decisions, and its ability to predict academic success have been studied extensively, both by the large research arm of the AAMC and by outside sources. While this information is generally available to the public, misinformation and misconceptions about the MCAT live on in internet forums and by word-of-mouth. We present five common misconceptions about the purpose of the MCAT and what it's testing.

#1 **The MCAT is a content test, summing up the courses I took in undergrad.**

Yes, the MCAT does contain a lot of content—eight semesters' worth of science (two semesters each of physics, general chemistry, organic chemistry, and biology). This will only increase with the new MCAT 2015 (all of the courses needed for the current MCAT,

Chapter 1

Why Was the MCAT Created? (And What's It All About?)

K

plus a semester each of biochemistry, psychology, and sociology). But while you need to know the Doppler effect, the Henderson-Hasselbalch equation for buffers, acyl substitution reactions, and the hormones that govern the menstrual cycle (sometimes called the HPO, or hypothalamic-pituitary-ovarian axis), content alone is *not* sufficient for excellent MCAT performance. Rather, **critical thinking—the ability to reason, to integrate, to look at a problem in a creative way and find efficient methods to solve it—is the primary driver of a high score.**

Why is this? Well, schools can get a sense of your content knowledge by looking at your undergraduate or postbaccalaureate grades. But the thinking process and ability to *use* these sciences is not tested evenly across schools; thus, the MCAT acts as a great equalizer, testing your ability to *think*—and not just *memorize*. And perhaps most importantly, critical thinking underlies your ability to succeed as a physician. Consider the patient coming into the emergency department with acute abdominal pain of four hours' duration. Sure, you could memorize all of the possible diagnoses, work-ups, and treatments for every condition that causes abdominal pain ... or could you? The differential diagnosis (list of likely causes) is extensive; but considering the age of the patient, the patient's gender, comorbidities (other illnesses he or she has), and the description of the pain, you can reason what questions would be best to ask to decide on the diagnosis.

MED SCHOOL INSIGHT

In some medical schools, students play "100 Causes of Abdominal Pain." And there really are at least a hundred: everything from abdominal aortic aneurysm (AAA, an enlargement—and potentially a rupture—of the aorta in the lower back) to a Zuckerkandl organ pheochromocytoma (a particular epinephrine-producing tumor located outside the adrenal gland). How could you choose which diagnosis is correct for a patient *without* critical thinking?

#2 The MCAT likes to test the exceptions, the unusual examples, the esoteric content.

This is a common misconception of the MCAT, which leads many premedical students to take additional coursework that is *not* necessary for success on Test Day. While advanced inorganic synthesis, anatomy and physiology, and modern physics can show up in an MCAT passage, the outside knowledge required by the AAMC still adheres to the eight-semester sequence previously mentioned.

It's certainly not a bad idea to take more advanced science courses if your schedule permits—an understanding of anatomy and physiology before you get to medical school will undoubtedly make cadaver dissection a bit easier—but recognize that these courses should not be taken *specifically* for the MCAT. All the information necessary to answer the questions will be in the passages, or in outside knowledge as listed by the AAMC's content outlines.

FIND MORE ONLINE

The AAMC content outlines list the outside knowledge students are expected to know before taking the current MCAT. These lists are narrower than many students expect; note the absence of rotational inertia or momentum, alkene reactions, and phylogeny.

Chapter 1
Why Was the MCAT Created? (And What's It All About?)

So why does it feel like the MCAT is asking questions you've never seen before? Remember—it's all about critical thinking: the MCAT is a master of testing basic material at a high level, especially by integrating the various sciences with each other. For example, the MCAT could explain the cardiovascular system as a group of parallel resistors, and apply circuit properties to our understanding of heart failure, hypertension, and sepsis.

#3 Passages are included on the MCAT to slow me down.

Students sometimes assume that passages are included as background information for those unfamiliar with the content covered in a given set of questions. Therefore, they misinterpret the passages as merely introducing a time crunch, rather than being a critical part of the test.

The change to passage-based questions in 1992 came from a far more sophisticated drive than timing: they require you to integrate new information with the corpus of knowledge you already have, and see how they jive together. MCAT passages will frequently challenge common assumptions about a given scientific process, or introduce an experiment testing the validity of a scientific idea. Only by reading the passage and actually *seeing* what happens can you be prepared for the accompanying questions.

Medicine is a field requiring continuous learning. Our advancements in technology belie our advancements in understanding the human body. Much like you will have to integrate new information with what you already know while reading MCAT passages, you will have to stay abreast of the newest studies in medicine through academic journals, conferences, and trainings. Admissions committees (and your future patients!) are very interested in your ability to adjust to new data, to manipulate it, and to absorb it into your schemata of how the world works.

#4   I'll never use this information again—especially as a doctor!

The concepts and critical thinking that underlie the MCAT are *both* important to decisions you'll make as a doctor. We've discussed the critical thinking, but why are these concepts important? There's probably no better way to prove it than a few examples.

When a patient breaks a bone, the translational forces and torques still acting on the bone can be used to predict what structures might be damaged if the fracture is angulated or displaced (moved from its starting position). We also must understand these forces and torques if we are to reset the bone correctly.

Acid and base chemistry dictates the blood disturbances we see in everything from chronic obstructive pulmonary disease (COPD) to altitude sickness, to acute kidney failure. We further use the principles of acid-base chemistry and the semipermeable membrane to increase the excretion of toxins; a patient with an overdose of aspirin (acetylsalicylic acid) can excrete more of the toxin when it is *deprotonated* since it takes on a negative charge and thus cannot cross the cell membrane to reenter the body from the renal tubules. Urinary alkalization (when titrated correctly) can therefore help avoid a toxic overdose.

The continuity equation and Bernoulli principle explain the pathophysiology of a number of valvular and vascular disorders in the body. In fact, one of the diagnostic findings in valvular stenosis (the narrowing of a heart valve) is an increased velocity of bloodflow. Physicians know from the continuity equation that as cross-sectional area decreases, velocity increases (assuming a constant flow rate/ cardiac output).

Isomerism is a critical consideration in drug design. Consider the proton-pump inhibitor omeprazole (used for gastroesophageal reflux disease, peptic ulcers, and other acid-excess states). When this medication was going to come off patent, a new drug was developed: esomeprazole. Take a look at the names there. Omeprazole is a

Chapter 1
Why Was the MCAT Created? (And What's It All About?)

racemic mixture; esomeprazole is only the *S*-enantiomer of the same drug. Yet the receptor here is achiral! Thus, for a huge difference in cost, the patient sees very little difference when taking one drug versus the other. Yet a patient be thankful when the therapy you prescribe doesn't break the bank!

There are hundreds of additional examples. But, to be clear, drawing out these connections between science and medicine, and making them more explicit, is a critical component of MCAT 2015.

#5 The MCAT is not particularly predictive of my success in medical school.

While it may have been a bit harder to draw a correlation between your SAT score and success in undergrad, **the MCAT has been demonstrated multiple times to be highly predictive of first- and second-year grades in medical school and success on the United States Medical Licensing Examination, Step 1 (USMLE, or the "Boards")**. A landmark study by Ellen Julian in 2005[4] found that the MCAT was 59% correlated with first- and second-year grades, 46% correlated with clerkship (third-year) grades, and 70% correlated with Step 1 scores. This was significantly higher than undergraduate GPA alone, at 54%, 36%, and 49%, respectively. The brief takeaway: dominating the MCAT bodes well for your success in medical school.

All in all, the MCAT has come a long way from its creation as the Moss Test in 1928. And as it continues to evolve in the 21st century, it remains a challenging—yet valid!—test. Together, we'll master the MCAT, whether you take the current version or MCAT 2015. With that, let's see what's actually changing in the new exam.

---

4 Julian ER. Validity of the Medical College Admission Test for predicting medical school performance. *Acad Med.* 2005; 80(10): 910–7.

CHAPTER 2

What MCAT 2015 Will Look Like

You bought this book to get a better sense of what MCAT 2015 is going to look like. While AAMC-written practice exams will be released in 2014, the AAMC has provided a wealth of information through their *Preview Guide for the MCAT[2015] Exam*.[1] This document can be a bit dense to read, however, so we've distilled the major structural, content, and scoring highlights of the new exam.

Section	Science Topics	Number of Questions	Number of Minutes
Biological and Biochemical Foundations of Living Systems	Biochemistry (25%) Biology (65%) *Remaining 10%: General and Organic Chemistry*	67	95
Chemical and Physical Foundations of Biological Systems	Biochemistry (25%) General Chemistry (33%) Organic Chemistry (15%) Physics (25%) *Remaining 2%: Biology*	67	95
Psychological, Social, and Biological Foundations of Behavior	Psychology (60%) Sociology (30%) Biology (10%)	67	95
Critical Analysis and Reasoning Skills	None. All information necessary to answer the questions is contained in the passages.	60	90

---

1 At the time of writing, the most recent version of the *Preview Guide* is version 2, released in September 2012. Check AAMC.org/mcat2015 for more recent editions of, or updates to, the *Preview Guide*.

TEST LENGTH AND SECTIONS

MCAT 2015 will have four sections. Since the section names are quite long, we're providing some abbreviations that you'll see used throughout this book:

- Biological and Biochemical Foundations of Living Systems (Bio/Biochem)
- Chemical and Physical Foundations of Biological Systems (Chem/Phys)
- Psychological, Social, and Biological Foundations of Behavior (Psych/Soc)
- Critical Analysis and Reasoning Skills (CARS)

Each of these sections is longer than their current MCAT counterparts, with the three science sections containing 67 questions each (up from 52 on the current MCAT), which are allotted 95 minutes of testing time. The CARS section will be 60 questions (up from 40 on the current MCAT), which are allotted 90 minutes of testing time. This represents an increase of almost two hours of testing time (6 hours, 15 minutes).

The order of these sections is *not* yet definitive; there have been some conflicting reports from the AAMC about the sequence in which they'll be presented.

MCAT FACTS

The MCAT 2015 will consist of 6 hours, 15 minutes of testing time—an increase of almost two hours from its current form. Timing and stamina will be crucial skills for success on Test Day.

The major addition to MCAT 2015, as far as sections go, is Psychological, Social, and Biological Foundations of Behavior. Students will be asked questions that cover knowledge often taught in first-year psychology and sociology courses.

CHAPTER LINK

Check out Chapter 7 for a more thorough breakdown of the new content appearing on MCAT 2015.

PASSAGES AND CONTENT

Passages will now be written to test science concepts *in the context of living systems*. In other words, gone are the days of a passage, describing a roller coaster car descending a track at an angle θ, with a given height h and coefficient of kinetic friction μ_k that is accompanied by questions asking for plug-and-chug application of these principles. Rather, solution chemistry could be tested as an underlying theme in our understanding of urolithiasis (the formation of kidney and bladder stones); organic oxidation and reduction mechanisms as a component of the metabolism of toxins like ethanol; and atomic absorption and emission spectrometry as it relates to bioluminescence.

The AAMC has not yet announced how many passages will be contained in each section, but it is likely to increase from the current number of seven. All indications show that there will still be a 3:1 ratio of passage-based questions to discrete questions (questions not associated with a passage).

As aforementioned, the new MCAT will cover quite a bit more content than it did in previous versions of the test. The recommendations, as made by the AAMC, include two semesters each of physics, general chemistry, organic chemistry, and biology; one semester each of psychology, sociology, and biochemistry; and an understanding of statistics and research design. Note that, while it is not given its own section, biochemistry, which previously had a minimal appearance on the MCAT, will make up a full 25% of Bio/Biochem.

MED SCHOOL INSIGHT

Of all of the sciences assessed by the MR5 Committee (discussed in Chapter 3), biochemistry was deemed to be the most important competency for entering medical students to have. This is connected to an increased focus, as a community, on molecular medicine, treatments that can be personalized, genomics, and epigenetics—all of which have biochemistry and an understanding of biomolecules at their core.

QUESTIONS AND SKILLS

A full-length MCAT 2015 will contain 261 questions, which are divided into four Scientific Inquiry and Reasoning Skills (SIRS). While these skills are further explained in Chapter 11, it is worthwhile to note here that there will be a greatly increased number of questions focusing on research design and bias (Skill 3), as well as data interpretation and statistical analysis (Skill 4). These previously made a minimal appearance on the MCAT, but will not constitute a significant proportion of the questions—perhaps even up to one-third, combined between the two skills.

A TIMELINE OF THE TEST CHANGES

Given how different MCAT 2015 will be, it is useful to keep yourself updated with the latest materials released by the AAMC and Kaplan. Here is the AAMC's timeline of past and future events related to the new MCAT.

- **November 2011:** First *Preview Guide for the MCAT2015 Exam* released.

- **September 2012:** Second *Preview Guide for the MCAT2015 Exam* released. All questions from the first *Preview Guide for the MCAT2015 Exam* were scrapped in the writing of this newer version.

- **January 2013**: The first administrations of the current MCAT *without* the Writing Sample, and *with* the Trial Section (see Chapter 1).
- **Late 2013 to early 2014**: The final version of the *Official Guide to the MCAT^{2015}* should go live. This will replace the *Preview Guide for the MCAT^{2015} Exam* to become the definitive document outlining the structure, content, and style of the new test.
- **Spring 2014**: The first AAMC-written MCAT 2015 Practice Test will be released.
- **January 2015**: The last administration of the current MCAT; the second AAMC-written MCAT 2015 Practice Test will be released.
- **Spring 2015**: The first administrations of MCAT 2015 will begin.
- **Summer 2015**: The first students with scores from MCAT 2015 will begin applying to medical school, and will matriculate in **August 2016**.
- **2017 to 2018**: The last opportunity to apply with pre-MCAT 2015 scores; the AAMC has stated that it will stop releasing pre-MCAT 2015 scores during one of these two application cycles.

CHAPTER 3

Why the MCAT Is Changing

If the current MCAT is already well-studied and known to be highly predictive of medical school success, why does it need to be overhauled?

MCAT 2015 comes at a time when the face of healthcare is changing; the exam itself merely reflects a much larger pattern of reform. As we consider the roles of physicians and patients, of inpatient and outpatient treatment, of insurance and compensation, and of preventative care and health maintenance, the MCAT similarly must adapt to train physicians of the future.

CHAPTER LINK

See Chapter 4 for information on how the changes to the MCAT may affect the future of healthcare.

For now, we consider the "nuts and bolts" of the three major changes in the MCAT 2015: adding Biochemistry and Psychological, Social, and Biological Foundations of Behavior; restructuring the other sciences to be presented in biologically-based passages; and increasing the length of the exam.

CHANGES IN CONTENT

Biochemistry

The drive for biochemistry, like all of the changes in MCAT 2015, has its roots in the MR5 (MCAT Review #5) committee recommendations. Delivered at the 2011 AAMC meeting, these fourteen points were assembled after a rigorous analysis of advisory committees' input; over 2700 surveys from administrators, college and medical school professors, residents, and students; and myriad outreach events.

The majority of the survey asked faculty, residents, and students how important they felt certain topics were in the current curriculum, as well as how important they felt those topics would be in a future medical curriculum. The findings were quite interesting. **Biochemistry was rated the most important science for students to master for the medical school curricula of the future** (average score 3.34 on a five-point Likert scale, with 5 being the highest). Six of the top-ten-rated topics in the survey belonged to the related field of cell and molecular biology. So it's clear that biochemistry is considered important for the medical student of the future.

Psychology and Sociology

Given the expanding diversity in American society, our interconnectedness during the digital age, and the aging of the patient population, there has been an increasing focus in medical schools on cultural sensitivity. Further, many of the top causes of morbidity and mortality in the United States are caused by behavioral and environmental determinants of health: smoking and drug use, diet and exercise, and inequities in care due to socioeconomic status.

MED SCHOOL INSIGHT

Many medical schools assess the cultural sensitivity of their students through standardized patients (SPs). SPs are actors hired to mimic signs and symptoms of disease, who also give feedback to students on their interpersonal and communication skills. Working with SPs during the preclinical years allows students to practice interviewing, examining, and advising patients even before they hit the wards.

While behavioral sciences actually fell in last place in the MR5 survey (average score 2.39), this may be reflective, in part, of a lack of awareness of the behavioral sciences among current medical students and residents. Support for the importance of this material came from the *Behavioral and Social Sciences Foundations for Future Physicians* report, published in November 2011. Three main themes were identified for why this material should be included in the MCAT. First, the diverse theoretical frameworks used in the behavioral and social sciences underscore the importance of thinking through "complex (and often chaotic) systems"[1]—like the biopsychosocial model—to understand the patient. Second, the strong connections to research methods and data analysis in these fields align well with the testmaker's goal of increasing questions on these topics and the need for medical students to design and critically analyze research, as part of evidence-based medicine. Finally, the content of psychology and sociology is a welcome addition to a medical student's fund of knowledge.

FIND MORE ONLINE

For more insight into the addition of psychology and sociology to MCAT 2015, check out the AAMC's *Behavioral and Social Sciences Foundations for Future Physicians* report.

---

1 Behavioral and Social Science Expert Panel. Behavioral and Social Science Foundations for Future Physicians. AAMC. 2011.

BIOLOGICALLY-BASED PASSAGES

How often have you wondered to yourself—while cramming for that organic chemistry or physics final—"Why do I need to know this as a doctor?" Many premedical students question the relevance of some of the material on the MCAT.

The support for the material on MCAT 2015 comes from the MR5 survey, as previously detailed. But the presentation of this content is changing as an answer to this question of relevance. Rather than testing thermodynamics through a gas-piston system, which fails to demonstrate why a doctor would actually need to understand these principles, why not present it in a passage on the proper treatment of frostbite (slow rewarming through a convection current in a rotating water bath at 40–42°C)?

Some schools are better than others at establishing these connections for students; integrated and clinically-based courses are extremely helpful with this goal. But by making this application of hard science in a biological context a top priority, MCAT 2015 can increase this exposure among students even *before* they arrive for their white coat ceremony.

A LONGER (AND MORE POWERED) EXAM

The greatly increased length of MCAT 2015 (261 questions in 6 hours, 15 minutes testing time—up from 144 questions in 3 hours, 20 minutes testing time) actually reflects its use in admissions decisions. Historically, the total score was the most important for admissions committees; section subscores in Physical Sciences, Verbal Reasoning, and Biological Sciences merely showed the breakdown in this score so schools could pick up on students who were highly lateralized toward one section. That is, while two students could each have a 30, a breakdown of 10-10-10 would be interpreted quite differently than 15-10-5.

CHAPTER 4

Medicine: Now and in the Future

In Chapter 3: Why the MCAT Is Changing, we explored the actual changes to the MCAT, and got a sense as to the research behind adding biochemistry, psychology, and sociology to the exam; the new passages that will test all sciences within a biological context; and the increased number of questions and total testing time.

Here, we will look at the exact same concepts, but put them into the larger picture of how medical education—and medicine itself—is evolving. This chapter is meant to be a fun read, but it should also make you think about what role *you* want to serve in the future of medicine and beyond. Consider what you're passionate about and what drives you to be an excellent doctor.

CHANGES IN CONTENT

Biochemistry

As medical technology advances, we are able to look ever closer into the human body. Whereas diagnoses in the early 20th century were made predominantly by gross specimens and histology (examination of cells under the microscope), we are now able to look within the cell to the organelle and, indeed, to the molecular level.

Laboratory science now underlies most medical decision making: approximately 60 to 70% of diagnostic and treatment decisions, admissions, and discharges are based on laboratory tests.[1] And this makes sense. With increasing precision and objectivity, physicians are able to determine exactly the cause of a patient's pathology and tailor treatments to that problem.

MED SCHOOL INSIGHT

While most medical decisions are rooted in some form of laboratory testing, it is not effective medicine to just order as many tests as possible for a patient. In medical school, you'll learn about the effective use of lab tests to arrive at the correct diagnosis, without subjecting your patient to unending needle sticks.

Consider the success of a drug like imatinib mesylate (Gleevec). Its predominant use is in chronic myelogenous leukemia (CML), a blood-borne cancer most commonly associated with the "Philadelphia chromosome." This genetic aberration is a fusion between chromosomes 9 and 22, which brings two genes, BCR and Abl, near each other. This BCR-Abl product is a tyrosine kinase that is constitutively activated—that is, permanently turned on. BCR-Abl can then add phosphate groups to tyrosine amino acids in various proteins, promoting the cell cycle and causing cancer. Well, knowing that BCR-Abl would make an excellent target for treatment, imatinib was created to block the protein's function. Survival rates of patients with CML improved significantly, as did rates of complete cytogenetic response (all cells testing normal, without the Philadelphia chromosome). By identifying a molecular target and designing medications to treat this very specific protein, exceptional treatments with reduced side effects became possible.

Further, how many of the major causes of morbidity and mortality in the United States are based on biochemical principles? Diabetes

---

1 The Value of Clinical Laboratory Services. American Clinical Laboratory Association. 2007.

mellitus (type 2) is one of the most common chronic diseases in the U.S., and its effects contribute to almost every one of the top ten causes of death in this country. The illness itself has its roots in biochemistry: the primary feature is the improper metabolism of glucose due to insulin resistance and, eventually, decreased production of the hormone. Severe insulin resistance, as it turns out, affects more than just glucose; other disturbances of metabolism include high levels of acid in the blood from ketone bodies and shifts in potassium levels. The long-term consequences of diabetes are due to biochemical pathology as well. Advanced glycation end products (AGEs) are formed as glucose sticks onto otherwise normal molecules throughout the body, eventually leading to coronary artery disease, strokes, and kidney failure. Many other major diseases are also understood through complex biochemical pathways, including hyperlipidemia and hypercholesterolemia (high fats and cholesterol in the blood, respectively).

The future of medicine will be reliant on molecular diagnostics and therapy, as well. Since the Human Genome Project originally sequenced the genome in 2000, science has come to discover the causal (or, at least, *a* causal) gene for many inherited or complex conditions. By genotyping a tumor, scientists and physicians can predict how effective various treatments will be—and perhaps, as with Gleevec, create new therapies for that specific disease. This concept of personalized medicine is already hot within the medical community, and is poised to be the future of effective treatment.

MCAT FACTS

Of all the sciences, biochemistry was rated the highest in importance for entering medical students to know in AAMC's survey of medical faculty, residents, and students. So now it makes up 25% of the material in two sections of the test (Bio/Biochem and Chem/Phys).

Psychology and Sociology

There are three major trends at play that are changing healthcare needs and the patient population in the United States. First, the increased diversity in the population as a whole (from immigration, increased social and academic mobility, and interconnectedness through technology) puts physicians in front of patients whose thoughts and beliefs about health and well-being may be starkly different than their own. Second, increased access to healthcare through reform legislation has allowed millions of patients to reach providers for the first time. Finally, successes in medicine and public health have increased the survival from many formerly fatal conditions and have enabled people to live longer. This leaves the United States with an aging population, where individuals may be coping with multiple illnesses simultaneously.

To arm physicians of the future with the skills needed to take care of this population, many medical schools are increasing their coursework in interpersonal skills ("Doctor-Patient Relationship," "Doctoring," or "Physician, Patient, and Society" at various schools), as well as cultural competency and research ethics. This is part of the "biopsychosocial model of medicine," a term coined in a 1977 *Science* article that posits that illness is due not only to molecular, mechanical, or structural disturbances within the body, but also the mentality and environment of the patient. Perhaps discussions in these courses could be more advanced—more focused on the *application* of behavioral science principles—if students arrive already familiar with this material. Therefore, the role of Psychological, Social, and Biological Foundations of Behavior is not just to test you on additional content knowledge from Psychology 101 and Sociology 101, but to assess your sensitivity toward the issues that your patients—whose cultures may be vastly different than yours—cope with daily. And further, how do those patients *behaviorally* deal with that stress? As mentioned in Chapter 3, many patients' health problems are due in part to their vices and behavioral responses to life stressors: smoking, substance abuse, self-destructive behaviors, and others.

There is a sense that familiarity with the behavioral sciences and strong interpersonal skills will help create a more empathetic physician. One of the most important attributes to hone before starting medical school is an ability to just listen and interpret. One study demonstrated that the average time a patient spoke at the beginning of a primary care appointment before being interrupted by a resident physician was only 12 seconds.[2] Patients want to be listened to. Multiple studies have shown that patients' satisfaction with their doctors (usually assessed by patient satisfaction surveys) is highly correlated to their sense of being heard. This is easy to do in theory—sit when talking to the patient, maintain eye contact, reflect back what the patient says, and respond appropriately to their body language—but not always easy in practice. As patient appointments necessarily get shorter and as care plans increase in complexity, what will you do as a medical student, resident, and physician to maintain this rapport with your patients?

Finally, behavioral sciences are such a critical part of American medicine because they underlie a physician's ability to counsel patients. Unlike the old model of "doctor knows best" (often referred to as the "paternalistic" approach to medicine), today's doctors work *with* patients to find solutions to their health problems. Patients now come to their doctors armed with information (and sometimes misinformation) from online chat rooms, social media, and the lay press. The interpersonal skills trained in medical school, coupled with the understanding of the inner workings of the mind and society tested on MCAT 2015, are necessary to effectively work with patients to change behavior, find appropriate and tolerable treatment plans, and thus improve health outcomes.

MCAT 2015 is, of course, not the only way medical schools will try to predict your bedside manner and ability to empathize with patients—that's very much the purpose of the medical school interview as well. It's all about your ability to communicate clearly and effectively with others. Medicine is, at its core, a humanistic practice of care

2 Rhoades DR, *et al.* Speaking and interruptions during primary care office visits. *Fam Med.* 2001; 33(7): 528–32.

for one's community. To be a successful physician, you will have to be able to bond with patients whose belief patterns differ from your own, debate with colleagues whose practice of medicine differs from your own, and work in teams whose members' roles differ from your own.

MCAT FACTS

In a 2011 Kaplan survey, **87% of medical school admissions officers supported the changes implemented in the new MCAT.** Further, 73% stated that they believe these changes will better prepare premedical students for medical school.

FIND MORE ONLINE

Check out *Kaplan Test Prep's 2011 Survey of Medical School Admissions Officers* for more information on how important the MCAT is in the admissions process.

BIOLOGICALLY-BASED PASSAGES

Medicine has evolved from a descriptive science to a prescriptive and mechanistic science. What exactly does this mean? Whereas doctors of the past thought through illness by describing the associated symptoms and physical findings, they now spend most of their time trying to understand *why* and *how* an illness developed. This ties into the "zooming in" of medicine to the molecular level as previously described, and will allow physicians to develop therapies that do not just treat the *symptoms* of the illness, but fix the underlying mechanism.

Consider the current protocols for using respirators in patients with acute respiratory distress syndrome (ARDS). When the lungs cannot function, the body cannot get enough oxygen, and thus carbon dioxide cannot be released. Traditionally, treatment of ARDS would require ventilating the lungs enough to correct these blood gas derangements. This necessitates lots of positive pressure, stretching the lungs large enough to diffuse these gases over a larger surface area. However, the lungs are governed by physics: stretching the lungs this much exceeds the functional spring constant of lung tissue (Hooke's Law), causing small breaks in the tissue and promoting scarring. Even the makeup of the inhaled gas is important. Counterintuitively, it is *not* best practice to give 100% oxygen to ARDS patients for prolonged periods. Oxygen can produce free radicals and oxidize tissue (redox reactions), leading to even more scarring. And since oxygen is freely diffusible across the cell membrane and the gradient promoting the flow of oxygen from lung into blood is always there, all of this oxygen can be absorbed. This sounds good, but it leaves almost no gas in the alveoli, which then collapse due to surface tension. By keeping some nitrogen in the inhaled gas, the alveoli are held open (Dalton's law of partial pressures) and can permit more gas diffusion.

Only by understanding the underlying physics, chemistry, and biology that contribute to this and many other disease states were scientists able to come up with more effective protocols for treatment, which increased survival and positive outcomes and decreased time spent in the hospital.

A LONGER EXAM

This may be the hardest aspect of the exam to justify being a part of the future of medicine, but it's certainly part of *your* future in medicine. Almost all of the standardized exams you'll take as a medical student and beyond, like the United States Medical Licensing

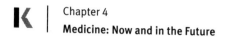
Exams (USMLE, or the "Boards") and residency in-service exams, include at least seven to eight hours of testing time. Having taken MCAT 2015, you'll already have a leg up on preparing for other similarly extended exams. And of course, working on your academic stamina will help you with those late nights on call.

Now that we've taken a look at the large-picture changes in the MCAT and why they're occurring, let's take a more specific look at what the content changes will look like. Over the next few chapters, we explore what's staying the same (Chapter 5), what's going away (Chapter 6), and what's being added (Chapter 7) to the test.

CHAPTER 5

What Will Stay the Same

Reading the official *Preview Guide for the MCAT²⁰¹⁵ Exam* might give the impression that the new exam will simply manifest out of thin air. In that guide, the AAMC doesn't talk much about today's MCAT at all, even though it's a logical reference point for many test takers. We argue that it's useful to examine MCAT 2015 through the lens of the current MCAT, which will be administered through January of 2015. After all, the MCAT has existed in more or less its current form for over 20 years, so the content of the exam has become common knowledge in the premedical community.

If you're somewhat familiar with the current form of the MCAT—for instance, if you have friends or relatives who have taken the MCAT recently, or if you've taken it yourself—you'll find this chapter, and the two following it, especially useful. We'll first cover what will stay the same between the exams (Chapter 5), then we'll cover what is being removed (Chapter 6), and then what's being added (Chapter 7).

Even if you're not familiar with the current exam and will be completely new to the MCAT in 2015, you should stick around anyway. In these three chapters, we'll cover most of the major details of MCAT 2015 to some degree, so either way you will learn a lot that will help you succeed when you take the test yourself.

THE CURRENT PREMEDICAL CURRICULUM IS STILL IMPORTANT

The current version of the MCAT is an outgrowth of an age-old interplay between the demands of medical schools and the corresponding reactions of undergraduate premedical programs: medical schools ask for certain knowledge and skills from applicants, so premedical programs (and postbaccalaureate programs) incorporate courses that teach that knowledge. The MCAT, then, is the standardized measure that stands between the undergraduate curriculum and the medical school curriculum; it tests whether students actually learned that content to the level that medical schools require.

MED SCHOOL INSIGHT

One trend in medical school admissions today is a gradual shift away from defined prerequisite courses. While most schools still require a transcript with the classic four years of science, some have custom relationships with local undergraduate institutions that supersede prerequisites, while others are moving toward a "competency-based" admissions model that is looser about required classes. Some have even abolished prerequisites altogether. Remember, though, that the MCAT will be the same no matter what happens to prerequisite courses, so no matter what science courses you've taken, make sure you thoroughly review and practice all the MCAT science topics before taking the exam.

The medical school prerequisite curriculum for sciences, known so well to premedical students, is:

- Two semesters of biology
- Two semesters of general chemistry
- Two semesters of organic chemistry
- Two semesters of physics

While some medical schools expect a little more than this—many expect at least a semester of biochemistry, for instance—these eight semesters probably represent the core of what you're currently studying (or have studied). The important takeaway from this is that the AAMC has decided not to take anything out of this recipe. **MCAT 2015 will still test science knowledge across all eight semesters of the classic premedical curriculum.**

CHAPTER LINK

See Chapter 9 for information on scheduling the prerequisite curriculum, as well as a discussion of the *nonscience* medical school prerequisites.

IMPORTANT POINT

The science material encompassed by the classic premedical curriculum is still very challenging, and it will require just as much hard work to master for the MCAT in 2015 as it always has. Don't discount the importance of the four classic sciences, because they will still contribute greatly toward your MCAT 2015 score.

MCAT 2015 will also require knowledge from *all new* prerequisite courses: psychology, sociology, and biochemistry. These three new topics will make up almost half of your total MCAT 2015 score. But we'll have more on that later; for now, the major point is that you will still need proficiency with college-level biology, general chemistry, organic chemistry, and physics to succeed on MCAT 2015.

CHAPTER LINK

See Chapter 7 for more detailed information on the new prerequisite sciences that will appear on MCAT 2015.

(ALMOST) ALL THE CURRENT SCIENCE TOPICS ARE BEING KEPT

This point is similar to the last, and it goes along with a major theme: the revision to the MCAT in 2015 is not so much a test *change* as it is a test *expansion*. In other words, the vast majority of changes to the test are additions, and there are very few subtractions.

This means that if you have an older sibling who studied for a pre-MCAT 2015 administration—even if it was 20 years ago—almost everything that he or she studied will also apply to your MCAT 2015 experience. Specifically, **all of the following topics are on the current MCAT and will also appear on MCAT 2015:**

CHAPTER LINK

The topics marked with an asterisk (*) will be tested in a slightly different capacity on MCAT 2015 than they are in the current exam. See Chapter 6 for how exactly these topics will be changing for MCAT 2015.

Biology

- Cell (Eukaryotic and Prokaryotic) and Virus Structure
- Enzymes
- Cellular Metabolism
- Reproduction
- Embryology
- Organ Systems
  - Musculoskeletal System*
  - Digestive System
  - Respiratory System
  - Cardiovascular System
  - Lymphatic & Immune System

- Skin System
- Excretory System & Homeostasis
- Reproductive System
- Endocrine System
- Nervous System

- Mendelian Genetics & Heredity*
- Molecular Genetics
- Evolution*

MCAT FACTS

Even though the four science subjects cover roughly equal numbers of topics within them, this *does not* mean that all science topics have equal weight in your final MCAT 2015 score. On MCAT 2015, biology (at 65% of the Bio/Biochem section) will be by far the most important of the four "classic" MCAT subjects, followed in importance by general chemistry (33% of the Chem/Phys section); physics (25% of the Chem/Phys section); and finally organic chemistry (15% of the Chem/Phys section).

General Chemistry

- Atomic & Molecular Structure
- The Periodic Table
- Bonding & Chemical Interactions
- Stoichiometry
- Chemical Kinetics & Equilibrium
- Thermochemistry
- Gases
- Solutions
- Acids & Bases
- Redox Reactions
- Electrochemistry

Organic Chemistry

- Basic Organic Compounds & Nomenclature
- Isomerism
- Stereochemistry
- Hybridization & Bonding
- Alcohols
- Aldehydes & Ketones
- Carboxylic Acids
- Carboxylic Acid Derivatives
- Separations & Purifications (Laboratory Techniques)
- Spectroscopy*
- Biological Molecules

  - Carbohydrates
  - Amino Acids
  - Proteins
  - Lipids

Physics

- Units & Kinematics
- Newtonian Mechanics*
- Work & Energy*
- Thermodynamics
- Fluids (Statics & Dynamics)
- Electrostatics
- Circuits*
- Light & Optics
- Sound
- Atomic Phenomena

  - Absorption & Emission Spectra
  - The Photoelectric Effect

- Nuclear Phenomena
- Radioactivity
- Nuclear Binding Energy

SCIENCE AND STRATEGY WILL BE TESTED IN COMBINATION

The MCAT has always tested science knowledge in a unique way. Throughout the last 20 years of MCAT history, answering a science question correctly has required a combination of preexisting science knowledge, reasoning and critical thinking skills, and test-taking strategy. For example, a question in the Physical Sciences section of the current MCAT might require you to remember a physics formula, ask you to identify the correct numbers from the passage to plug in to that formula, and give you a couple of stand-out trap answer choices that could be eliminated immediately by an experienced test taker.

These science questions that demand both outside knowledge and test-taking skills are here to stay, and they will be just as prevalent on MCAT 2015 as they are on today's exam. The AAMC has even explicitly identified which Scientific Inquiry and Reasoning Skills they will test on MCAT 2015; you can use this information to your advantage in your preparation for the test.

CHAPTER LINK

For an explanation of the Scientific Inquiry and Reasoning Skills that MCAT 2015 will test, check out the first half of Chapter 11.

"VERBAL REASONING" IS NOT REALLY CHANGING MUCH

The current MCAT has a 60-minute, 40-question **Verbal Reasoning** section that tests your ability to read and analyze samples of graduate-level writing in the humanities, natural sciences, and social sciences.

MCAT 2015 will have a 95-minute, 60-question **Critical Analysis and Reasoning Skills** (CARS) section that tests your ability to read and analyze samples of graduate-level writing in the humanities and social sciences.

MCAT FACTS

The "CARS" acronym for the Critical Analysis and Reasoning Skills section of the exam might sound a little silly, but it is actually the official abbreviation used by the AAMC.

Those two descriptions should sound very similar, because they are. The takeaway is simple: besides the change in name, the lengthening of the section, and the removal of natural science-themed passages, **the CARS section of MCAT 2015 will be essentially identical to the Verbal Reasoning section of the current exam.**

TEST DAY TIP

The Verbal Reasoning/CARS section of the MCAT famously requires no outside knowledge to answer questions correctly; all the information needed to answer the questions can be found by combining information in the passage with well-developed analytical skills. For this reason, the removal of natural science-themed passages for MCAT 2015 will not have a significant impact on the strategies and skills that you will use on the CARS section.

It is worth clarifying, however, that this doesn't mean that the CARS section will be easy or "throwaway" by any means. Even on the current MCAT, the Verbal Reasoning section is the hardest section for many test takers, due in part to the very short time period it gives them to read such complex passages and perform such sophisticated reasoning. None of these difficulties will go away on MCAT 2015, so succeeding on the CARS section will still demand the discipline that comes along with systematic practice and proven strategies.

THE TEST IS STILL EXTREMELY IMPORTANT

Even though much about the MCAT is changing in 2015, it is still a supremely important exam for your educational and professional career, and your performance on the test will still heavily influence your future as a medical student and as a physician.

While the significance of the test may seem daunting, it's also critical to remember that **the importance of the MCAT is actually good news**! The high-stakes nature of the MCAT means that if you prepare thoroughly and ace it, you will really distinguish yourself within the large pool of medical school applicants. Although this has always been true about the exam, the more challenging MCAT 2015 means that the opportunity is even greater for hardworking students to stand out from the crowd and achieve their ultimate goal: acceptance to medical school.

CHAPTER 6

What Will Be Removed

As noted in the previous chapter, the 2015 test change is mostly a test *expansion*; quite a lot is being added, but very little is being removed. However, "very little" is not quite "nothing," and this chapter is where we'll cover the small list of features that are on the current MCAT but won't be on MCAT 2015.

IMPORTANT POINT

This is not an exhaustive list of items being removed for the 2015 test change; for instance, MCAT 2015 is also losing the current MCAT's optional trial section (which has always been unscored and therefore inconsequential) and the natural science–themed passages on its Verbal Reasoning/CARS section (which doesn't change Verbal Reasoning or CARS strategies because the section doesn't require outside knowledge). However, subtractions beyond those on this list shouldn't influence the way you prepare and study for MCAT 2015, so we won't go into detail about them.

A FEW LOW-YIELD SCIENCE TOPICS ARE BEING REMOVED

For MCAT 2015, the AAMC has decided to eliminate a few science topics. Only they know exactly why they've chosen these topics to eliminate, but the implication is that these topics are no longer as relevant to success in medical school as they once were.

Practically speaking, a lot of the changes seem to be happening to accommodate the small reduction in physics questions for the new exam. But whatever the reason for it, **these are the topics that MCAT 2015 will no longer test:**

TEST DAY TIP

Just because these topics aren't listed in the AAMC's *Preview Guide for the MCAT²⁰¹⁵ Exam* doesn't mean you should ignore these topics in your science courses, or that you "shouldn't worry about them." As a premedical student, you should appreciate that all science is connected, and you never know when these topics will surface in medical school or in your career as a physician. (It's also true that the AAMC is technically allowed to change their test requirements at any time, so you may end up seeing them on the MCAT after all.) So remember to take these deletions as "facts about MCAT 2015" rather than "topics that aren't important to my life anymore."

General Chemistry

- Phase equilibria removed
  - Exception: phase diagrams still tested

Organic Chemistry

- Several compounds no longer directly tested
  - Simple organic compounds (alkanes, alkenes, alkynes)
  - Aromatic compounds
  - Ethers
  - Amines

Physics

- Momentum removed
- Solids (density, elastic properties, etc.) removed
- Periodic motion (springs & pendulums) removed
  - Exception: Spring potential energy still tested
  - Wave characteristics (amplitude, beat frequency, etc.) removed

---

MCAT FACTS

Some of these organic chemistry topics were actually removed from the current MCAT years ago. However, this removal was a slow process, and there is still some general confusion about whether or not they are on today's MCAT. This is why we're reiterating these removals here. It's also worth noting that knowledge of the general properties and names of these organic compounds will still be useful as components of higher-level questions on MCAT 2015.

CERTAIN SCIENCE SUBTOPICS ARE BEING ALTERED

In addition to the few science topics that will be removed entirely (see aforementioned), MCAT 2015 will test certain topics less intensively than the current MCAT does. Most of these alterations, however, are quite small. Here are the **changes in science subtopics for MCAT 2015:**

Biology

- Musculoskeletal System—Bone growth & bone generation removed
- Mendelian Genetics & Hereditiy—Pedigree analysis removed
- Evolution—Origin of life removed

General Chemistry

- No topics substantially altered

Organic Chemistry

- Carboxylic Acid Derivatives—Acyl halides removed
- Spectroscopy—Mass spectrometry removed
- Separations & Purifications—Recrystallization removed

Physics

- Newtonian Mechanics—Circular motion removed
- Work & Energy—Center of mass removed
- Circuits—Alternating current removed

MCAT 2015 WILL HAVE (SLIGHTLY) FEWER PHYSICS QUESTIONS

Having done some number-crunching on the information released by the AAMC, Kaplan has noticed something interesting about the frequency of science subjects to be tested on MCAT 2015, especially in its Chemical and Physical Foundations of Biological Systems (Chem/Phys) section. Take a look at the following table for the approximate number of questions per science subject on the current MCAT (on the left) versus the corresponding number for MCAT 2015 (on the right). Pay special attention to the row for physics, about halfway down:

Science Subject	Total Number of Questions (Today)[1]	Total Number of Questions (2015)[1]
Biology	39	52
General Chemistry	26	25
Organic Chemistry	13	14
Physics	**26**	**17**
Psychology	0	40
Sociology	0	20
Biochemistry	0	33
Verbal Reasoning/ CARS	40	60
Total	**144**	**261**

You will notice that biology's share increases dramatically and both chemistry topics are kept about equal to their current level, but there is a marked decrease in the number of physics questions that

---

1 Question distributions are approximate, as there will be small deviations from administration to administration. Rollup totals (the bottom row) are exact, however.

will be on MCAT 2015. Don't get too excited though. This does *not* mean that the breadth of physics tested on the exam is much smaller (see earlier in this chapter for the short list of topics being removed); all it really means is that the MCAT 2015's assessment of your two semesters of college physics will be spread out over a somewhat smaller number of items.

CHAPTER LINK

If you're planning to take the MCAT in early 2015, you may have the opportunity to choose whether to take the current MCAT or the new MCAT 2015. But don't jump to a conclusion on which test to take based solely on the number of physics questions; instead, go to Chapter 15 of this book for a full analysis of the "Which test should I take?" question.

CHEMISTRY AND PHYSICS WILL BE TESTED ONLY IN THE CONTEXT OF LIVING SYSTEMS

This is perhaps the most interesting "removal" of the 2015 test change. For a long time, MCAT test takers have experienced passages and questions that are very much like what they've seen in their college science courses: physics passages about ski slopes and chemistry questions about test-tube reactions, for instance, have been very commonplace.

According to the AAMC's *Preview Guide for the MCAT²⁰¹⁵ Exam*, MCAT 2015 will no longer test physics or general chemistry outside the context of biological systems. This means that the days of ski slopes and test tubes are over, and on MCAT 2015 you're more likely to see physics passages about skin conductance, and acid-base chemistry questions about stomach acid and blood buffer systems.

CHAPTER LINK

If you're wondering what questions like this will look like, check out Chapter 12 of this book for some sample physics and chemistry questions in the MCAT 2015 style.

At the end of the day, it is important to remember that the test-makers are undergoing this monumental change in the MCAT so test takers can understand and integrate the complexities of basic science into their future careers as physicians. We at Kaplan support them in this goal not only because of its implications for the future of healthcare, but also because this change may actually make it *easier* for students to study for the physics and chemistry portions of the MCAT. For years, we've known that Kaplan students find clinical correlates—the real-world medical applications of MCAT science topics—to be one of the most interesting and engaging parts of their test preparation. And starting with MCAT 2015, the only way you will be tested on physics and chemistry is through those very same clinical correlates. For all the parts of the test change that might make you anxious or stressed, this is one that just might put a smile on your face.

CHAPTER 7

What Will Be Added

In this chapter, we'll finally cover the details of the biggest news about the test change: what's new! If you wait just a few short months between January of 2015 and spring of 2015 to take the MCAT, you'll see many content- and structure-based details in the spring that you wouldn't have seen in January. Let's cover them one by one.

THE BEHAVIORAL SCIENCES SECTION ("PSYCH/SOC")

The most-publicized change to the MCAT 2015 is, of course, the addition of the Psychological, Social, and Biological Foundations of Behavior section. This new section is more commonly called the "Psychology/Sociology" or "Psych/Soc" section (this is the name we'll use), the "Behavioral Sciences" section, or the AAMC's preferred abbreviation, "Foundations of Behavior."

CHAPTER LINK

If you haven't already, check out Chapter 3 of this book to find out why the MCAT is changing, and why the AAMC is adding the behavioral sciences section at all. Then, if you need a mood-booster, read Chapter 4 to see why we should all be a little happier in a world with an MCAT that tests these sciences.

According to the AAMC, the new Psych/Soc section will consist of approximately 67 questions over 95 minutes, and it will cover the science subjects of psychology (60% of the section), sociology (30%), and biology (10%). In their preliminary blueprint, the test makers have revealed that the behavioral sciences content to be covered is generally what is taught in one semester of introductory psychology and one semester of introductory sociology (known in many undergraduate course catalogs as Psychology 101 and Sociology 101). The 10% of the section that is devoted to biology, on the other hand, will be drawn from the same year of biology instruction that is required by the Bio/Biochem section—it's the portion of that content that is most relevant to perception and behavior, which makes it a better tie-in to Psych/Soc.

More specifically, here are the major topics that will be tested on the Behavioral Sciences section. You'll notice that these topics are presented in a different way from those in the Chem/Phys and Bio/Biochem sections (in Chapter 5, these were listed strictly by science subject). That's because the AAMC is taking an especially functional view of the behavioral sciences in their test blueprint, and most of the topics on the new section will be tested in a "blended" way between multiple science subjects. So we'll follow their example and organize these by Content Categories, the AAMC's name for these groupings. The science subjects associated with each Content Category will be signified with letters after the category's name: **P** for psychology, **S** for sociology, and **B** for biology.

FIND MORE ONLINE

As with all of our information about the blueprint of the MCAT 2015, this list of topics comes from the AAMC's *Preview Guide for the MCAT 2015 Exam*. If you would like to see that information in further detail, you can download the Preview Guide yourself by visiting https://www.aamc.org/students/applying/mcat/mcat2015/.

Sensing the environment **(P, B)**

- Vision, hearing, and other senses
- Perception

Making sense of the environment **(P, B)**

- Attention
- Cognition
- Consciousness
- Memory
- Language

MCAT FACTS

These science-subject designations are not meant to be proportional; for instance "Making sense of the environment," labeled "**(P, B)**," isn't evenly divided between psychology and biology (it happens to be overwhelmingly psychology-focused, with just a little biology)—the "**(P, B)**," in this case just means that the Content Category has psychology and at least some biology within it.

Responding to the world **(P, B)**

- Emotion
- Stress

Individual influences on behavior **(P, B)**

- Biological Influences on Behavior
- Personality
- Psychological Disorders
- Motivation
- Attitudes

MCAT FACTS

The biology found in Psych/Soc is limited to the areas of biology most relevant to behavior and psychology. The bulk of this consists of the structure and function of sensory organs and the nervous system (eyes, ears, brain lobes, etc.), but it also includes the biological causes and effects of stress, psychological disorders, and other psychological phenomena.

Social influences on behavior **(P, S)**

- How the Presence of Others Affects Individual Behavior
- Group Processes
- Culture
- Socialization

Attitude and behavior change **(P, B)**

- Habituation and Dishabituation
- Associative Learning (Classical & Operant Conditioning)
- Observational Learning
- Theories of Attitude and Behavior Change

Self-identity **(P, S)**

- Self-concept and Identity
- Formation of Identity

Social thinking **(P, S)**

- Attributing Behavior to Persons or Situations
- Prejudice and Bias
- Processes Related to Stereotypes

Social interactions **(P, S)**

- Elements of Social Interaction (Statuses, Roles, Networks, etc.)
- Self-presentation and Interacting with Others

- Social Behavior (Attachment, Aggression, etc.)
- Discrimination

MCAT FACTS

Remember that the AAMC has reserved the right to change the specific topics and subtopics that will be tested on the MCAT 2015. Given the substantial investment in these topics on the part of the AAMC—they've been writing items already for a while now—there is unlikely to be a dramatic change. Even so, be aware that the test blueprint may change slightly between now and the spring of 2015.

Social structure **(P, S)**

- Theoretical Approaches
- Social Institutions
- Culture

Demography **(S)**

- Demographic Structure of Society
- Demographic Shifts and Social Change

Social inequality **(S)**

- Spatial Inequality (e.g., Residential Segregation)
- Social Class
- Health Disparities
- Healthcare Disparities

That's quite a long list, isn't it? However, if you've taken some psychology and sociology, then hopefully you're already familiar with some of these concepts. On the other hand, if these are completely new to you, then it's best to speak with your pre-health advisors and faculty to find out how you can best learn these subjects given your school's curriculum.

MED SCHOOL INSIGHT

The medical school community has not decided whether to add the two semesters of behavioral sciences (and one semester of biochemistry) as formal prerequisites for admission in the 2015–2016 admissions cycle and beyond. But while some schools may make the courses prerequisite, **many medical schools will probably allow you to prove your psychology and sociology skills through MCAT 2015, without requiring that you take the associated college courses**. While this means your MCAT 2015 score could hold even more weight in the admissions process, it could also mean that your undergraduate course schedule becomes much more manageable.

Here are a few more facts about the new section, gleaned from the information and practice questions released by the AAMC:

1. **Psych/Soc is very much a science section,** and it will demand knowledge of the formal teachings of psychology and sociology just as intently as the Chem/Phys and Bio/Biochem sections will demand knowledge of the science covered in those sections. A common misconception is that Psych/Soc is "just another Verbal section," but it really isn't.

2. **Many passages and questions on Psych/Soc will revolve around a study and the results of that study**. These passages will give the new section plenty of chances to include Skill 4 questions, which represent the MCAT 2015's focus on data analysis. This also means there will probably be very few "information" passages on new section, and that most questions will demand application of scientific principles to novel situations, rather than simple recall of those principles.

3. **Psych/Soc will heavily test your knowledge of experimental and research design.** Based on information the AAMC has released, we suspect that Psych/Soc will test Skill 3 more intensively in this section than the other science sections will. That means that your knowledge of experimental design, dependent versus

independent variables, representative sampling, and ethics in research, among other things, will really be put to the test in the context of the behavioral sciences.

CHAPTER LINK

See Chapter 11 for more information and sample question stems on Skill 3, Skill 4, and the other science and verbal skills to be tested on the MCAT 2015.

And finally, it's worth noting that **we at Kaplan are already hard at work preparing for this new section**, and we have been since the AAMC released their first *Preview Guide for the MCAT^{2015} Exam* in 2011. When it comes time for your test, we'll be more than ready to help you ace Psych/Soc, and we'll have plenty of section-specific practice and strategies to help you succeed on the new section.

CHAPTER LINK

See Chapter 12 for sample problems on all four sections of the MCAT 2015, including Psych/Soc.

BIOCHEMISTRY

When combined with the material from Psych/Soc, biochemistry completes the suite of new science material that the MCAT 2015 will test. Biochemistry will be tested on both the Chem/Phys and the Bio/Biochem sections, and the new biochemistry material will make up approximately 25% of each of those sections.

IMPORTANT POINT

Even though the word "biochemical" appears only in the name of the Bio/Biochem section, biochemistry will also be tested on the Chem/Phys section, and the subject will have equal weight (25%) in each of those two sections.

Biochemistry, taken as a whole, is a very large body of content, so it's very important to know exactly to what extent it will appear on MCAT 2015. There's no need to guess at specifics, however, because the AAMC has outlined exactly which biology and chemistry topics on MCAT 2015 will also demand knowledge of biochemistry. This list purposefully coincides with what is taught in a single-semester undergraduate course on the subject. **These topics are listed below, organized by the test section on which they will appear.**

Chemical and Physical Foundations of Biological Systems (Chem/Phys):

- Acids & Bases
- Ions in Solutions
- Separations & Purifications (of biological molecules)
- Biological Molecules (structure, function, and reactivity)
  - Nucleotides, DNA, and RNA
  - Amino acids, peptides, and proteins (including protein folding)
  - Lipids
  - Carbohydrates (disaccharides and polysaccharides)
  - Phenols and other aromatic compounds
  - Bioenergetics
  - Kinetics
  - Mechanisms

MCAT FACTS

You may notice that some of these topics, such as proteins and cellular metabolism, overlap with some of the biology, general chemistry, and organic chemistry topics from Chapter 5. When this is the case, it means that the MCAT 2015 will be testing these topics as they are covered in *both* courses. So, for a topic like protein structure, you'll need to know not just the general principles of three-dimensional protein folding (from biology), but also the specific reactions and bonds, such as disulfide links, that bring about that structure (from biochemistry).

Biological and Biochemical Foundations of Living Systems (Bio/Biochem):

- Biological Molecules (definitions and biological functions)
  - Amino acids
  - Carbohydrates
  - Proteins (including enzymes)
  - DNA and RNA
- Bioenergetics
  - Definition and principles
- Metabolism
  - Breakdown of glucose, fatty acids, and proteins
  - Citric acid cycle
  - Oxidative phosphorylation
  - Hormonal regulation of metabolism
- Plasma Membrane Structure & Mechanisms
- Biosignalling

CHAPTER LINK

This chapter provides a simple list of all the new topics to be tested on MCAT 2015. If you'd like to know what steps you need to take for your own MCAT 2015 success, look to Chapter 9 for test prep advice and Chapter 10 for guidance on what to do if you don't have a plan to take the new courses.

TEST DAY IS GETTING (A LOT) LONGER

This very important point can be summarized in one chart. We saw a similar chart back in Chapter 2, but this is a side-by-side comparison of today's MCAT versus MCAT 2015.

Section Name		Number of Questions		Time Spent (minutes)	
Today	2015	Today	2015	Today	2015
Physical Sciences	Chem/Phys	52	67	70	95
Verbal Reasoning	CARS	40	60	60	90
Biological Sciences	Bio/Biochem	52	67	70	95
(Trial Section)	Psych/Soc	(32)	67	(45)	95
Whole Exam[1]		144	261	3 h 20 m	6 h 15 m

---

1 "Whole exam" excludes both the trial section for current MCAT (because it's unscored) and all breaks, tutorials, and surveys for both exams as their lengths will vary between test takers and have not yet been finalized for the MCAT 2015.

CHAPTER LINK

Remember that these section names are not the AAMC's official section names for MCAT 2015. You can find the full section names in Chapter 2, but they're very long and somewhat impractical—unless you're a true perfectionist, don't worry about committing them to memory. Also, recognize that the sections for MCAT 2015 are out of order in this chart; they're merely aligned with the section they most resemble in today's MCAT.

This extended Test Day length is a very big deal, and one common reaction to it is, "That's not fair!" But as with so many other parts of the MCAT, it's important to approach it with a positive, practical attitude. With that in mind, here are some concrete facts about what this longer test means for you as a test taker:

1. **Mental stamina and endurance** will be even more important than they are now. Endurance has always been an important test-taking skill, but maintaining focus over time will become an absolute necessity for the MCAT 2015.

MCAT FACTS

This long-form MCAT is not unprecedented. The old pencil-and-paper version of the MCAT, which was administered through the end of 2006, was about as long as the MCAT 2015 will be.

2. **Smart management of your full-length exam practice** will be extremely important to proper preparation for the MCAT 2015. Since practicing a full-length exam will take a full day, it simply can't hold the same place in your studies that a shorter exam would have. Practicing a full-length MCAT 2015 will have to be a special, preplanned event in your study schedule, and you'll have to balance it with plenty of other personalized skill- and stamina-building practice.

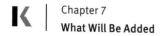

3. **All of your competition will be taking this same extra-long test.** The MCAT has always calculated its scaled scores, based on percentile ranking. So even though the MCAT 2015 is sure to be more challenging due to its length, that spike in difficulty may actually help you score *higher* if you're well-prepared for it and other test takers aren't.

MED SCHOOL INSIGHT

Your medical licensing exams (USMLE Step 1, Step 2 CK, Step 2 CS, and Step 3), which are the standardized tests you'll take during and after medical school, will all be at least as long as MCAT 2015. Step 1 and both parts of Step 2 are each a full day of testing, and Step 3 is *two* full days. So the good news is that all of your stamina training for the MCAT 2015 will pay off for years to come.

CHAPTER 8

Ask a Psychometrician

One of the keys to building good practice material is making sure that it is psychometrically sound. Kaplan recently sat down with one of our psychometricians, Sylvia Tidwell Scheuring, to get her take on MCAT 2015.

So Sylvia, what exactly is a psychometrician? What do they do?

A psychometrician basically is responsible for determining whether the questions on an assessment, or test, are in fact measuring the construct that the assessment is intended to measure. We work on tests of any kind: content tests, like the MCAT, and psychological tests in which we determine what people's attitudes are. The idea is that you're measuring what's going on inside the human brain and you're trying to figure out what someone knows, what someone's able to do, or how someone looks at the world. Basically, we need to use a lot of statistics and large samples to get that information. So, we deal with lots of people to figure out how the content is interacting with each individual person and then aggregate the results.

What is your background?

Well, I started out in Physics—Radiation Physics—teaching students at the junior college level. Then I transitioned into building artificial intelligence systems for a number of years where I became interested in using artificial intelligence in education by designing and developing assessments for one of the largest testing companies, CTB/McGraw-Hill. Since then, I've done consulting—doing psychometrics—trying to understand what students know and what they don't know, and how to help them get from where they are to where they want to go. At this point, I have probably analyzed the performance of *millions of students*—everything from kindergarten to medical school.

How can your analysis help students improve their performance on tests like the MCAT?

Historically, the MCAT is what we call a norm-referenced test—that means you're being compared to other people, not just to yourself. It's not like the state assessments that you take when you're entering 12th grade. Specifically, the MCAT is different because what they [the AAMC] want to do is compare you to all the other students who are taking the MCAT. Therefore, knowing how other students are doing in certain areas can help you to determine "Am I as good as most students in this area? Am I better than most students in this area?" This means that strength and weakness is actually different than you would expect with tests like the one given in lower grades (criterion-referenced tests) where what they are testing is if you know the content or "meet the standards." For the MCAT, what you actually want to know is "Am I good enough to get in where I want to go?" That's a question of "How do I know that I'm going to be at that level, and if I'm not at that level, what areas am I weak in that I need to be stronger in?" Psychometric data and analysis can provide those kinds of answers to students and the people who help students prepare for these exams.

How will the questions on the MCAT and its scoring reflect that norm referencing?

What it means in terms of questions is that there are some harder items on the MCAT than most people can answer. In fact, you can expect that the range of difficulty on items in the MCAT will go from questions that most people would get right to questions that almost no one would get right. Ultimately, the goal is to be able to separate out the higher performance students from the nonhigher performance students from the medium performance students from the lower performance students.

With respect to scoring, scales for tests like the MCAT are defined against the mean of performance for students. We figure out how many standard deviations your performance is off of the mean, convert that to a z-score which is then converted to your scaled score in the test, which is an arbitrary score. At this point, I'm not sure what the scale is going to be for the new MCAT, however.

Why is that? Do you think that the AAMC will change the scoring for MCAT 2015?

Actually, yes. Most testing companies change the scale when they release a brand-new test and alter the fundamental construct. The reason it is a totally different scale is to make sure people understand that the assessment doesn't measure the same thing it did before. Test-makers usually don't want confusion with the reporting and hence they do not want the scale to overlap with the previous scores so people don't get confused between scores from the old test and the new test.

So aside from the possible change in scoring, what do you see as the principal differences between the current MCAT and MCAT 2015?

The biggest difference is that they [the AAMC] changed the construct that's being measured. It used to be measuring just biology, general chemistry, organic chemistry, physics, and verbal reasoning. Now they've added psychology, sociology, and biochemistry to that list. The AAMC has essentially extended the domain significantly; instead of just having to take introductory basic science courses, you're going to need to take sociology, psychology, and biochemistry before taking the MCAT. Not only is that a lot, it will also make an impact on your overall test score since, according to my analysis, as much as 46% of MCAT 2015 may be testing these new constructs.

In addition to that, the test is significantly longer. It will be about six plus hours, which means that students will spend longer answering test questions under high stress.

Finally, the test makers are focusing a great deal more on analysis and reasoning skills as well as incorporating data into your decision making. Therefore, students can expect a lot more reasoning as opposed to recall expectations for this new test.

Given the new constructs and other challenges on MCAT 2015, how do you recommend students use practice materials that the AAMC releases?

Since the test-maker has only released the *Preview Guide for the MCAT²⁰¹⁵ Exam* and won't even release the first practice test until 2014, it is going to be really challenging for students. I would really save those items that they present for practice in the study guide for testing (don't look at the answers!) rather than trying to figure out what they're testing. That is, try to take the questions and actually answer them after you've done the studying—after you've actually learned the content—because that will tell you if you're learning at the level that they're expecting you to. Since there are so few of those questions, if you just look at them first they're not going to be a good measure of the whole domain on each test. If you look too broadly at the topic, then you may fall into the trap of "Well, I'll just make sure I learn that particular thing during the course" and unfortunately that is not an accurate sample. So it would be best if you learned the content by reading the descriptions of the content in the *Preview Guide for the MCAT²⁰¹⁵ Exam*, and then look at the questions after you've learned the content and ask "Am I learning at this level or not?"

So do you think that the practice materials that the AAMC releases—present and future—are the most test-like examples available in terms of both content and structure?

They're probably the most test-like in terms of the kinds of questions they're going to be asking and the way they're going to ask them, but they probably shouldn't be used to find out what all of the questions will cover. If you want to understand the domain of questions that will be covered, you really need to look at the *Preview Guide for the MCAT²⁰¹⁵ Exam*. It says what is in scope and lays out any knowledge that you need to have. But there are fewer questions in that study guide than there will be on the test so you have to think about it as a sample of a sample. You really need to expand out well beyond that if you want to be doing well on the test. Also, you need to think about how the content areas integrate with each other because that's the other big difference in this assessment— they're looking more at integrating the content areas as opposed to treating them individually.

Are there trick questions on the test?

That's a question I get a lot from people. It is true that there are questions that probably most people can't answer; it's a norm-referenced test after all. But a trick question is a question that even if you have the content knowledge you still don't have a good chance of getting it right because you have to have something else other than the content knowledge to get it right. Trick questions are very, very rare on high-stakes tests like this. It would be very unlikely that you would see one. What will *feel* like a trick question though is content that's measuring just a little bit above your ability level. It will feel like a trick question because a couple of the answer choices will look awfully similar because you are almost, but not quite at the level of knowledge that is necessary for the question.

But remember, no one is interested in purposely putting true "trick" questions on an assessment because the value of predicting total domain knowledge from it will be diminished. In fact, the statistics are designed to weed trick questions out and content editors, content developers, and people who review the items are all attempting to make sure trick questions don't appear. The goal is to make the questions difficult for the right reasons.

You have done some analysis on the *Preview Guide for the MCAT^{2015} Exam*. Are there any particular passages or question types students should look out for on the new exam?

They're not significantly different from the current MCAT, except in the content they're measuring and the higher emphasis on diagrams, data of all kinds, tables, graphs, charts, and statistical information. Those kinds of things have become more emphasized than they were previously. It's not that they've changed the kind of questions that they're asking; they've just changed what they're asking about.

The important thing to note is that there will be more questions on experiments because that's what a future doctor can expect in medical school. You can expect a lot more "experiment A versus experiment B" types of questions because they want to test how students apply knowledge to information coming from an experiment.

And what would you say the most important test-taking skills that will lead to success on MCAT 2015 are?

Since tests are really designed to have integrated requirements, you can't really just have one skill and be successful. That being said, the most important thing you can do on a test is understand the question that's actually being asked and answer only that question. A lot of people trick themselves into answering the wrong question because they didn't actually read all the words in the question.

Also, I think you need to understand your own knowledge limits. If you understand what your current knowledge is, then you will be able to improve upon it and do well on an assessment. On the other hand, if you don't understand your knowledge limits, you don't use the information you get from measuring yourself appropriately. Therefore, unless you are consistently setting up questions for yourself and your own study groups or working with someone like Kaplan to help understand what your current state of knowledge is, and be honest with yourself, you can't improve. There is a really strong tendency for some people to say "I did well on those questions; I'll take more of those" as opposed to "I did poorly on those questions, so then I'll need to take more of those."

Students need to understand what it is they are not getting, look at the incorrect responses and try to figure out what they thought that was different from the correct information, and that led them to believe that incorrect choice was correct.

How can students recognize those wrong answer traps that they fall into most regularly?

The best way, of course, is to have explanations that you can look at to ask "Is this answer choice explanation similar to that one? Do I have a misconception that's just carrying across all of these items in the same domain?" The other thing to realize is that it may not be a misconception; it may be misreading content. Sometimes, people are not reading the questions closely and don't look at every single word in the question, and they end up answering a different question and choosing the wrong answer. So there are two reasons you can get the patterns of incorrect answers—one is because your content knowledge is lacking in some particular area and another reason is because you're actually not answering the questions being asked.

So understanding the question is one skill, and knowing your knowledge limits is another. Any other skills that will be important for success on MCAT 2015?

Pacing is going to be important on this test in terms of making sure that you're moving through the content at a rate that you could actually finish. Because if you have one small gap in your knowledge and you let yourself get stuck on a question trying to answer it, you are going to lose the opportunity to answer other questions correctly. Learn when to and when not to answer the question because without that distinction, you're not going to be able complete the test in a reasonable length of time. In fact, you're going to actually take away the time you needed to reason through questions you do have content knowledge in.

How would you recommend students prepare for the new pacing challenges of MCAT 2015?

Just as you wouldn't want to try running a marathon on the first day you start learning how to run, you don't want to take a test that is six hours long as your first exposure to the test. So I would recommend building up to the length of time that you're actually going to have to take the real assessment, just as you would build up to running a marathon—longer and longer sessions.

Does that mean that students should expect to take fewer practice tests studying for MCAT 2015 because it's such a long test?

Given the length of the test I suspect that they would probably end up taking fewer of them. It would probably be the exact wrong way to do it though. You probably should take *more* despite the psychological tendency to want to take fewer.

Let me give you an example. If I'm training for a 10K run, then the number of runs I have to do to get comfortable running 10K is smaller than the number of runs I would have to do to get comfortable running 26.2 miles. They are distinct problems. If you're going to have to get to the point of endurance of getting through a longer exam, you probably need to try doing it more. There is more content, and being confident that you've practiced the right amount will require you to take separate tests to get different content domains. You're also going to have to take tests where all the content is integrated because, as we've mentioned before, the testmaker is integrating the content in the new exam. So you need to take enough tests to feel comfortable with as many combinations as possible.

So if we have a longer test and we expect students should take more of them to get to that level of endurance, how long should students plan on studying for MCAT 2015?

When you think about it, the domain has almost doubled: there were only four content areas plus Verbal Reasoning in the original test and now there are seven plus Verbal Reasoning. That's almost twice as much to learn. And the content areas are distinct from each other, so you need to study each of them separately. This is just my guess based on the content domain size, but I would say something along five, maybe six months. Then, of course once you've actually extended the domain out that far, if you're studying one content domain at the beginning and don't see it again until the end, you're going to have some forgetting going on. That's going to require reinforcement.

That is certainly a lot to consider for MCAT 2015. For the students in school thinking about this test and taking the courses that they need to take to take this test, is it advisable to study for the MCAT while they're taking their undergraduate science courses?

I think it is actually. I think there's extreme value in thinking about the context in which you're going to use this information: the medical context, integrative thinking, and application of data. These are all of the same things that are going to be focused in the MCAT itself. Thinking about things in this way will actually help students do better in the course as well because the more connections you have, the more interconnections you have, the easier it is for you to follow even in the context of your own course.

The challenge will be getting access to questions that are test-like. If those are available, then actually adding them in the appropriate locations within the course would actually make a lot of sense. Honestly, it's going to require at least an organization like Kaplan to provide test-like questions because it's really a lot of work to try and do; it's just very difficult.

There is a certain population of students who are going to have the option to take the current MCAT or MCAT 2015. What you think about that?

Well, I think that's a very individual choice because if you happen to be extraordinarily strong in the new constructs as compared to your peers, then taking the new test might be a very good idea because it will help boost you above everyone else. However, if your strengths are in the older domains covered by the MCAT, you may well want to take the current MCAT since your performance is likely to be higher on that test. Also, if you get really fatigued from tests that are really long, you might want to take the current one because it's a lot shorter.

How would you prepare for MCAT 2015 if you had to take it?

Well, if I was preparing for MCAT 2015 I would probably be taking the classes right now that I'm going to be tested on, or at least some of them. And I would be doing exactly what I talked about earlier, which is looking at my course materials and the concepts of how that material's going to be thought about by the people who write questions for the MCAT. I would also want to understand how the content that I'm learning in each of my courses interacts with each other. I would look at biology, chemistry, and physics, their connections and how they actually work together to help me understand what's going on in the body. I would look at quizzing myself not only on what's going to be tested by my professor in my course, but also what's going to be needed for me to have a good solid foundation for medical school. I would spend a lot of time looking at experimental information. I'd look at research papers and try to understand them in the areas that I'm currently studying in school because that's going to be the kind of thing I'm going to have to do when I take the MCAT.

Besides their undergraduate courses and what the AAMC provides, where else would you recommend students go to help prepare for the kind of test the new MCAT in will be?

I would look at the kinds of content that are going to be covered in my first year in medical school. I'd look at the syllabi that they post on the net for first-year medical school classes and see what kinds of things they're going to be expecting me to know, and I would make sure that I have the basis of knowledge for being able to understand what they're going to be introducing at that point. It's true that I'm pretty obsessive about these kinds of things, but the reason these things were chosen to be on the test is because those are the things that the medical schools felt were really important foundations for those students who will be entering. In fact, if I had some friends who are in medical school, I would quiz them on all the stuff that they've had to remember from when they were an undergrad for their current courses. What did you use from this chemistry course for your first year of medical school? What did you use from this biology course for your first year in medical school? What was beneficial for you to have known? What did you have to go look back up because you'd forgotten it?

Are there any questions that we didn't ask that we *should* be asking about this new exam, and what would your response for those questions be? Did we miss something that we should be telling students about that would be good for them to know?

So, I think the one thing that I would have asked myself as a student (and which students should continue to ask) is how much time I should spend studying in concert with taking my courses—what's enough, and what is too much, and where that sweet spot is going to be. And I think the question I would continue to ask myself is "how?" At what point am I still gaining a good proportion of the content I'm learning, and at what point am I just not—perhaps I'm just overwhelmed, and I'm not getting anything anymore? And so I would continuously measure myself to see if my learning was actually being productive. Back off when it's not, because I think that you can get too deep in something and think that "more time is always better." Sometimes more calendar time *is* better because the brain takes time to actually integrate information; if you don't give it some down time, sometimes it doesn't integrate that information very well. What I advise my students is give it a couple of nights' sleep in between tough concepts, because if you don't give your brain some time to process and integrate the information, sometimes it's not actually gaining anything. It's just like exercise: if you do the same thing every single day, using the same muscles every day, sometimes it is actually is worse than leaving it alone for a little bit.

Sylvia Tidwell Scheuring is a consulting psychometrician for Kaplan Test Prep.

CHAPTER 9

Preparing for MCAT 2015

Now that you've read how a psychometrician would prepare for the MCAT, let's take a look at planning your schedule to get ready for the MCAT—regardless of the version you end up taking. **It is possible to take either exam and score extremely well, but you'll have to plan, starting today.**

Of note, make sure that you make an appointment with your premedical advisor *as soon as possible*. While we provide some general recommendations in this book, your advisor will undoubtedly be more familiar with the requirements of your school and will know more specifically which classes students have taken in the past. Regardless of the version you choose to take, start planning out your academic schedule now. You don't want any surprises down the line!

IMPORTANT POINT

Make sure that you make an appointment with your premedical advisor *as soon as possible* and start planning out your academic schedule now. You don't want any surprises down the line!

In this chapter, we take a look at the classes the AAMC's *Preview Guide for the MCAT2015 Exam* recommends. This chapter then makes the assumption that you have some time before you're taking the MCAT, and can plan out your courses for the next two years. If you're already further along in your studies (or if you've already graduated), make sure to check out Chapter 10: What if I Don't Have Time for the Prerequisites.

RECOMMENDED COURSEWORK AND SCHEDULING

In Chapter 5, we took a look at the coursework medical schools require before you matriculate to their institution. Let's take a look at the courses the AAMC recommends for both the current MCAT and MCAT 2015. You'll notice that most of these courses are similar and, while some courses are being added to prepare for MCAT 2015, no courses are technically being removed.

FIND MORE ONLINE

Check out the *The Official Guide to the MCAT Exam* and *Preview Guide for the MCAT²⁰¹⁵ Exam* for more information on the courses recommended by the AAMC as preparation for both the current MCAT and MCAT 2015.

Both the current MCAT and MCAT 2015 require one year (two-semester sequence) of physics, general chemistry, biology, and organic chemistry (8 classes total). The MCAT 2015 will *also* require one semester of introductory psychology, sociology, and biochemistry (11 classes total). All prerequisites for the current MCAT could be completed in two years by taking biology simultaneously with general chemistry one year, and organic chemistry simultaneously with physics the second year. Thus, even if you're currently a freshman, you might be able to complete the

Biology

Most medical schools require, and the AAMC recommends, a two-semester sequence in introductory biology as adequate preparation for the MCAT and medical school. These two courses should be scheduled during your freshman year of undergraduate study for a couple reasons. First, if you're not positive that medicine is the right path for you, biology is the science most clearly connected to the content physicians think about every day. Second, premedical students who are science majors (especially biology majors) will often have to take higher-level biology courses as part of their studies. Even if you're a nonscience major, consider taking higher-level biology courses during your undergraduate studies. While most schools do not require such courses, taking a course dedicated to anatomy and physiology, immunology, cancer biology, or microbiology will demonstrate the application of these biology principles in a clinical setting—and gives you a real boost in your preparedness for the first year of medical school.

Most biology on the MCAT is anatomy and physiology, and it tends to be tested in the context of when something goes wrong, as with disease. It is not uncommon for the MCAT to present a disease, describe its clinical signs and symptoms, and ask you to elucidate the pathophysiology (physiology that's gone wrong) that leads to these findings. This should make sense—it will ask you to integrate your knowledge of normal anatomy and physiology with other concepts in biology (classical and molecular genetics in diseases with Mendelian inheritance patterns, enzyme regulation in endocrine and metabolic disorders, and the cell cycle and cell division processes in cancer development).

The yield of the different sciences is very important. **Biology is the most heavily tested science on the current MCAT** (75 to 80% of Biological Sciences), **and will retain that title in MCAT 2015** (65% of Bio/Biochem, and small contributions to the other two science sections). Within biology, molecular biology (transcription, translation, and DNA synthesis), classical genetics (Punnet squares and patterns of inheritance) and anatomy and physiology (as previously described) are the highest-yield. Therefore, choose classes that will give you a strong foundation in these areas. These are also topics that will be especially important as preparation for medical school. Advisors and upperclass students can help you navigate the course options at your school to find the ones that best fit these needs.

IMPORTANT POINT

Biology is the most heavily tested science on the current MCAT (75 to 80% of Biological Sciences), and will retain that title in MCAT 2015 (65% of Bio/Biochem, with small contributions from the other two science sections).

General Chemistry

Most medical schools require, and the AAMC recommends, a two-semester sequence in introductory general chemistry as adequate preparation for the MCAT and medical school. It is very important to schedule these two classes during freshman year since they are prerequisites for organic chemistry and biochemistry.

The trick to making your general chemistry classes relevant for the MCAT is to look for themes and principles, and *not* to get caught up in math. Many undergraduate institutions' general chemistry courses focus on stoichiometric calculations, determining rate constants (k), or solving for concentrations in equilibrium expressions. The MCAT does have plug-and-chug questions, to be sure, but a calculator *cannot* be used on the test. Therefore, most questions that do require some math use relatively easy numbers and straightforward equations.

Consider the topic of the equilibrium constant. Any "K"—that is, K_{eq}, K_{sp}, K_a, K_b and K_w—is the same concept, just within a certain special circumstance (K_{sp} is the equilibrium constant for salt dissociation—a solid turning into soluble ions, K_a is the equilibrium constant for acid hydrolysis—an acid mixing with water to form a proton and conjugate base, and so on). Therefore, you shouldn't treat these topics as separate pieces of content. They are all set up the same way:

$$K_{anything} = \frac{[products]^{s.c.}}{[reactants]^{s.c.}}$$

where [products] and [reactants] are the concentrations of the products and reactants, respectively, S.C. is the stoichiometric coefficient of each species (the fancy word for the number showing up before the chemical in the balanced equation), and only gases and aqueous species are included. Further, all K values are affected by temperature and remain unchanged by catalysts. So why act like these are five different topics to know and understand? Consolidate your knowledge by finding these themes between concepts.

As another example, consider the myriad periodic trends covered in your general chemistry class. Ultimately, all periodic trends boil down to how much the nucleus attracts the element's electrons (referred to as the effective nuclear charge, Z_{eff}), or how much the element "loves on" its electrons. The more the nucleus "loves on" its electrons, the closer those electrons are pulled inward (smaller atomic radius). More energy would be required to remove one of those electrons (higher ionization energy). More energy would be released when adding an extra electron (high electron affinity). The element would pull electrons closer to itself when in a bond (higher electronegativity). It would be harder to get the electrons to flow (lower metallic character and conductivity).

Therefore, while studying general chemistry, focus on themes and trends rather than just the math. Not only is this more true-to-form of what the MCAT will test, but it also just makes the material more memorable for midterms and finals, as well as long-term. Since it may be a solid two years between when you complete general chemistry and when you take the MCAT, anything that helps you remember the material is certainly a good idea.

Organic Chemistry

Most medical schools require, and the AAMC recommends, a two-semester sequence in organic chemistry as adequate preparation for the MCAT and medical school. Organic chemistry is ideally scheduled during the sophomore year, since it is usually a prerequisite for biochemistry courses.

Organic chemistry is often taught (and tested) in a vastly different manner in undergraduate classes than on the MCAT. Most schools' organic chemistry exams are set up in the same style. They often open with a page or two split into two columns. In the left column, reactants and reaction conditions are given; the right column is a big open space in which you draw the predicted product. This is followed up by a few pages where a reactant and product are given, and you are expected to draw a reasonable reaction mechanism from one to the other.

But the MCAT tends to focus on the "why" of organic chemistry more than the "what." While taking your organic chemistry classes, *do* make flashcards of the various reactions. But strive to *understand* why a particular reaction occurs. That means understanding what makes a better nucleophile, a better electrophile, or a better leaving group. It also means recognizing oxidizing and reducing reagents, and being able to predict what changes might be seen in functional groups when exposed to such a reagent. For example, an aldehyde mixed with an oxidizing agent would sensibly form a carboxylic acid (aldehydes have two bonds between carbon and oxygen; carboxylic acids have three).

IMPORTANT POINT

Organic chemistry is the least heavily tested science on the current MCAT (20 to 25% of the Biological Sciences), and will retain that title in MCAT 2015 (15% of Chem/Phys and less than 10% of Bio/Biochem).

Use organic chemistry laboratory time to understand the use and functionality of the different techniques you're employing. The focus in spectroscopy (IR, ^{1}H-NMR, UV-Vis) and separation and purification techniques should be *why* someone would use a particular technique, what assumptions are made in using this technique, and how to interpret the results of that technique.

Finally, learning organic chemistry is indeed like learning a new language. You'll do the same thing in medical school, too. Therefore, the terminology of organic chemistry is important for the MCAT. It's not common to have questions asking directly for nomenclature on your MCAT, but jargon is used in passages and questions with the assumption that you can understand what's being said. Isomerism, for example, uses terms like structural/constitutional isomer, stereoisomer, conformational isomer, diastereomer, enantiomer, geometric isomer, epimer, and anomer. You need to understand what these terms mean and be able to use these terms accurately.

Like biology, keep the yield of this science in perspective. **Organic chemistry is the least heavily tested science on the current MCAT** (20 to 25% of the Biological Sciences), **and will retain that title in the new MCAT** (15% of Chem/Phys, and less than 10% of Bio/Biochem).

Physics

Most medical schools require, and the AAMC recommends, a two-semester sequence in introductory physics as adequate preparation for the MCAT and medical school. Physics can be taken during sophomore year, especially if you're trying to take your MCAT before the change in spring 2015; alternatively, it can be pushed to junior year to lighten your courseload during the first two years of your undergraduate studies.

Similar to general chemistry, many undergraduate physics classes are focused heavily on solving problems mathematically. Often they require calculus as well; the MCAT does not expect you to apply calculus at all during the exam. And while it's more common to have plug-and-chug questions in physics than general chemistry, they're still not the norm.

Even so, knowing all of the formulas relevant to the MCAT is indispensible to your success. The testmakers like to write questions that require you to incorporate content knowledge from vastly different areas, and being able to find the connections between concepts underlies your success in physics classes and on the MCAT. One easy way to organize this is by knowing the formulas forward, backward, and upside-down. More important than memorizing, again, is *understanding* the connection between these concepts. Just knowing $C = \kappa\varepsilon_0 A/d$ doesn't help you if you don't know what those variables mean (capacitance, C, is equal to the dielectric constant, κ, times the permittivity of free space, ε_0, times the area of the plates, A, divided by the distance between the plates, d).

Taking it one step further, we can start moving from one concept to another by linking equations in our mind. For example, velocity is change in displacement per time ($v = \Delta x/t$). Then, kinetic energy is related to velocity ($K = \frac{1}{2}mv^2$). Kinetic energy is related to potential energy ($U = mgh$ or $U = \frac{1}{2}kx^2$). The spring constant brings us to Hooke's Law ($F = -kx$), which is conceptually related to Young's modulus ($Y = \text{stress} \div \text{strain} = (F/A) \div (\Delta L/L)$). For the MCAT, you similarly must be able to move horizontally between topics, linking together electrostatics with kinematics, fluid dynamics with heat transfer, and Newtonian mechanics with thermodynamics. Create these connections during your undergraduate classes—this is what can make physics fun and memorable (really!).

PREPARING FOR MCAT 2015: BIOCHEMISTRY, PSYCHOLOGY, AND SOCIOLOGY

The three sciences listed here constitute the material that is being added to MCAT 2015. Even if you're pretty confident that you're going to take the current version of the MCAT, it's vitally important to have a "Plan B" in the event that you have to take (or retake) the MCAT in spring 2015 or later. While there are some ways to circumvent taking these courses and studying the material on your own, this should not be your primary strategy.

CHAPTER LINK

In the event that you aren't able to take biochemistry, psychology, and sociology by Test Day, in Chapter 10 we explore some strategies to still master this material and succeed on the MCAT 2015.

Biochemistry

Most medical schools do not require biochemistry for entrance to their institution, although many schools highly recommend it. For the MCAT, the AAMC recommends one semester of college-level biochemistry. Since both general chemistry and organic chemistry are usually prerequisites to biochemistry, you will likely have to take this course during the fall semester of your junior year as you prepare to study for the MCAT during spring semester of that school year.

Many students are nervous about biochemistry because of how intricate and detailed the subject matter is. But this shouldn't be a deterrent to you—the human body is just as complex (indeed, metabolism is essentially just the application of biochemistry to human physiology), and it's this complexity that makes medicine so interesting. This may flow out of the fact that many undergraduate biochemistry classes focus ostensibly on the memorization of reaction pathways. Glucose is converted into glucose-6-phosphate by glucokinase or hexokinase, which is converted into fructose-6-phosphate by phosphoglucose isomerase, and so on. This is one way of considering glycolysis, but it's not the way MCAT 2015 is likely to test this information.

Based on the examples in the *Preview Guide for the MCAT*^{2015} *Exam*, it seems that the AAMC is more interested in testing the larger-scale concepts behind biochemistry. Enzymology comprises a substantial portion of the list of content topics the testmakers provide. For metabolism, the main goal appears to be familiarity with the major pathways of glycolysis, fermentation, the citric acid (Krebs) cycle, oxidative phosphorylation and the electron transport chain (ETC), gluconeogenesis, the pentose phosphate pathway, and fatty acid oxidation. That is, a solid grasp of what types of biomolecules—carbohydrates, lipids, amino acids or nucleic acids—the pathways act on, as well as their major forms of regulation, should provide far more insight into how the MCAT will assess your knowledge of biochemistry than memorizing a bunch of reactions.

As you study biochemistry, look for these connections between the metabolic pathways and connect these concepts to the underlying enzymatic processes that are going on. From there, assess how protein structure can dictate function. By *vertically* integrating biochemistry (from the process to the enzyme to the kinetics), you'll be working the thought processes you need for Bio/Biochem as well as Chem/Phys (biochemistry will make up 25% of each of these sections). These skills will also serve you well as a physician.

Psychology

Most medical schools do not require psychology for entrance to their institution. For the MCAT, the AAMC recommends one semester of introductory psychology. Since psychology is not a prerequisite for any of the other premedical courses, you can choose to take it any time before the MCAT. However, we suggest taking psychology sooner as opposed to later in your college career—perhaps during fall semester of sophomore year. The reason you don't want to put off psychology is because of its connections to critical analysis of research. Psychology has its roots in strong research design, and creating a robust psychological study is actually quite difficult. Controlling for lurking variables, assessing for sampling and generalizability errors, and finding creative ways to present data are some of the major challenges of this line of research, and—as described later—will be a major part of MCAT 2015.

This introductory-level course should suffice for the material that you'll be expected to know on Test Day. The breadth of psychology material that the AAMC is adding for MCAT 2015 is vast, including everything from cognitive processes (development, attention, language, and perception) to behavioral models (attribution theory, discrimination, nonverbal communication, and attachment) to abnormal psychology (mood disorders, psychosis, and personality disorders). Therefore, the broadest introductory-level class you can take would be optimal, rather than taking multiple courses covering more narrow topics at a deeper level, such as abnormal psychology or developmental psychology.

If possible, a course that includes psychological research is best. The testmakers are increasing the number of questions on research design and methodologies, bias, experimental error, and other related topics (what are referred to as Skill 3 questions) in the MCAT 2015. They're also adding more questions on data interpretation, including reading graphs and tables, especially those with experimental error. Psych/Soc is the optimal place in the exam for the MCAT to increase the number of experiment-based passages. Therefore, a class that requires you to read and interpret research studies will be very helpful in preparing for MCAT 2015. Given the push toward evidence-based medicine, the ability to critically analyze a research study will also dictate your success at keeping up with the latest recommendations in medicine further along in your career.

MED SCHOOL INSIGHT

Medicine is truly a career of continuous learning. Medical students are often told when starting school that up to 25% of the information they learn in their first year will be deemed inaccurate by the end of their fourth year. No study has formally verified this idea, but the fact remains: Medicine is a constantly evolving field. Your ability to stay apprised of the latest research will play a major role in treating your patients with the standard of care.

Sociology

Most medical schools do not require sociology for entrance to their institution. For the MCAT, the AAMC recommends one semester of introductory sociology. Since sociology is not a prerequisite for any of the other premedical courses, you can choose to take it any time before the MCAT. However, it may be best to take it as soon as you've completed psychology, during spring semester of the sophomore year. By continuing with behavioral sciences in the same year, you can create connections between the material of psychology (studying the mind and behavior at the individual level, and how the individual interacts with society) and the material of sociology (studying the mind and behavior at the societal level, and how society interacts with the individual).

An introductory course in sociology should suffice for the material you'll be expected to know on Test Day. While the sociology material on the MCAT 2015 is quite broad in scope, the depth is not as great as for other sciences included on MCAT 2015. Much of sociology may make intuitive sense to you, but it's important to know how to translate that intuition into the terminology the testmakers will use on MCAT 2015. A basic sociology course will arm you with the terminology you need to comprehend material on Test Day.

IMPORTANT POINT

For the behavioral sciences (psychology and sociology), breadth takes preference over depth on the new MCAT 2015. Take introductory-level courses that expose you to all facets of these fields, rather than courses that focus on a more narrow, specific topic.

Like psychology, be wary of taking a course too narrow in scope. While many institutions offer introductory sociology courses focused on a particular topic (race relations, a specific ethnic group, social control), you want your knowledge base to be as broad as possible. Therefore, go for the most general course your school offers. This will give you a little taste of the wide world of sociology and get you more prepared for MCAT 2015.

A FEW THOUGHTS ON VERBAL REASONING/CARS

Most medical schools require two semesters of writing or English as adequate preparation for medical school. There are no formal recommendations of specific types of writing or English classes as preparation for the MCAT. Further, there is no outside knowledge required for this section; all information necessary to answer the questions is included in the passage.

So how do you prepare for Verbal Reasoning on the current MCAT, or Critical Analysis and Reasoning Skills (CARS) on MCAT 2015? The answer is simple: Read and think. This direction is intentionally vague, because you want to expose yourself to as much information (especially opinionated, potentially biased information) as possible. Read academic journals both in topics that you enjoy, and in topics you sometimes struggle with. Watch the news and critique the arguments of political pundits and the popular media. Question the validity of advertisements. Challenge your professors (tactfully!). By honing your skills in constructing an argument, you can start to *deconstruct* the arguments you'll see on Test Day.

On the MCAT, it's all about the author. Most MCAT passages are author-driven, so most questions are about the author's argument or opinion. So as you're practicing reading and thinking for Test Day, find the author's voice—even if it's neutral. Ultimately, getting the right answer on Verbal Reasoning or CARS is about finding this voice and staying in scope. If you do just those two things, you'll have pretty much everything you need to answer correctly.

IMPORTANT POINT

On the MCAT, it's all about the author. Most MCAT passages are author-driven, so most questions are about the author's argument or opinion. So as you're practicing reading and thinking for Test Day, find the author's voice—even if it's neutral.

Finally, start thinking like the test maker. You'll find that when you can think like the AAMC, you'll answer questions like the AAMC. If, while reading, you encounter an odd word, a difficult phrase, or a strange turn of ideas, you'll probably wonder why it's there. So will the test makers, and they will be more likely to ask you about it. Skills in critical reading and argument dissection will pay off in points, not only in Verbal Reasoning/CARS, but in the other sections as well.

CHAPTER 10

What if I Don't Have Time for the Prerequisites?

In Chapter 9, we explored making a course schedule during your undergraduate studies to align, as much as possible, your academic goals, admissions requirements, and MCAT 2015–recommended courses. Although you may have already decided when you'll be taking the standard prerequisite courses (two semesters each in biology, general chemistry, organic chemistry, and physics; two semesters of English or writing; and competency in calculus, demonstrated by completed second-semester calculus (integration, sequences, and series) or "testing out" with an Advanced Placement (AP) exam score) for medical school, you may not be planning on taking the three courses that will be added to MCAT 2015: biochemistry, psychology, and sociology.

We understand that there are many reasons that you cannot— or choose not—to take these new courses. Perhaps you've already graduated from college and are working or completing another degree before medical school and do not easily have access to (or time for) these courses. Or maybe you're a postbaccalaureate student preparing the other medical school prerequisites, but your program has not yet integrated biochemistry and the behavioral sciences into their coursework. Maybe you're an undergraduate student currently but, because of requirements for your major, you don't have three open spots for more courses. Finally, because most medical schools do not require you to have completed these courses, you might just be deciding that you'd prefer to self-study this information for MCAT 2015.

Regardless of your situation, we are committed to helping you succeed on any version of the MCAT you take. In this chapter, we start by exploring a few options on how to access this material. We then take a look at each of the new subjects for MCAT 2015 and dissect them a bit further to ask at what depth you must understand this material. For this question, we provide three critical thinking questions for each subject. The answers that accompany these questions demonstrate the level of detail to which you should know each subject to be adequately prepared for Test Day. These are not intended as practice problems; rather, they serve as a gauge for you to analyze whether the study materials you're using are covering the content in the proper amount of depth for you to be ready for MCAT 2015.

FIND MORE ONLINE

Check out everything Kaplan's doing to get ready, as well as more study and test prep tips online at Kaplan's MCAT 2015 homepage. Don't forget to sign up to receive updates about the new test; the AAMC reserves the right to change the format and content of MCAT 2015 before it goes live, so you want to stay apprised of any of these changes.

STUDY OPTIONS FOR THE NEW MATERIAL FOR MCAT 2015

No matter what option you choose to gain the knowledge and skills the AAMC will be testing with this new material, it's imperative that you *do* spend time learning it. This is especially noteworthy for psychology and sociology. As we discussed in Chapter 7, many students have been expressing the misconception that Psych/Soc is designed to be a second Verbal Reasoning/Critical Analysis and Reasoning Skills (CARS) section. This could not be further from the truth! While critical reading and critical thinking underlie *every* section of the test, Psych/Soc—like the other science sections—is also very content-heavy. In fact, every example question in the *Preview Guide for the MCAT²⁰¹⁵ Exam* under Psych/Soc requires at least one piece of content knowledge and many require you to know much more than that. Consider questions where the answer choices are all different theories (functionalism, conflict theory, symbolic interactionism, social constructionism, etc.). To answer such a question, you have to understand what each theory is and the subtle differences between them. In other words, unlike CARS, not all of the information necessary to answer the questions is contained within the passage. Further, while some students think of psychology and sociology as "softer sciences" that are possibly a bit more intuitive, MCAT 2015 is not testing them in this way. The testmakers expect you to know the actual definitions of the jargon used in behavioral sciences, to be able to discriminate between different models for the same phenomenon (language and cognition, social development, and so forth), and to recognize the molecular, cellular, neurologic, and psychiatric correlates for a number of common disorders.

IMPORTANT POINT

Many students have been expressing the misconception that Psych/Soc is designed to be a second Verbal Reasoning/Critical Analysis and Reasoning Skills (CARS) section. This could not be further from the truth! While critical reading and critical thinking underlie *every* section of the test, Psych/Soc—like the other science sections—is also very content-heavy. In fact, every example question in the *Preview Guide for the MCAT2015 Exam* under Psych/Soc requires at least one piece of content knowledge.

With that, let's consider some of the options for studying biochemistry, sociology, and psychology material for MCAT 2015. We list these options here in decreasing order of likeness to MCAT 2015; in other words, the top resources in the list not only provide you with the necessary content, but do so in a way that demonstrates how the material will be tested on the new exam. The bottom resources, while providing you with all the necessary content, should be supplemented by test-like practice passages and questions so you can see the application of this material within the context of MCAT 2015.

- **Kaplan Test Prep MCAT courses**—Because of the amount of research we've put into this major test change, we've been able to distill the information taught in most first-semester psychology and sociology courses, as well as college-level biochemistry, to just what you need to know for MCAT 2015. Our MCAT 2015 course will be released with plenty of time to prepare for even the first administration of the new exam in spring 2015. Whether you choose an on-site, in-person class; a live-online class; private tutoring; or self-study "on demand," you'll have access to all of the material in print form, as prerecorded videos, and as practice questions, quizzes, and full-length exams. Once you've taken your Mini Test, if you identify these new subjects as an area of opportunity for you to improve your MCAT score, you can prioritize this information early in your study plan using the analysis and tracking tools built directly into our course. If you're more of a self-studier at home using our retail books, these still provide a comprehensive review of the material you need for Test Day and access to online resources for practice.

CHAPTER LINK

Don't forget to take your Kaplan MCAT 2015 Practice Test! This is a valuable resource because the AAMC's first practice test for MCAT 2015 doesn't debut until 2014, with a second practice exam scheduled for release shortly before MCAT 2015 goes live. Access to the Kaplan MCAT 2015 Practice Test instructions are given in Chapter 13.

- **Local institutions, community colleges, and adult continuing-education courses**—Depending on where you live and the amount of time you have available, consider enrolling in a course at a local college or university. Many community colleges offer introductory courses in psychology or sociology. This is probably not doable if you're already enrolled in a postbaccalaureate program or are in the midst of completing your college degree and don't have space for these courses. However, this may be a great option if you've completed your undergraduate studies and are currently working during the day. Community college or adult continuing-education courses are often offered at night and can be very affordable. It may be more challenging to find college-level biochemistry offered at your local community college, but larger institutions in your area may permit community members to sign up for courses on a prorated basis. Check with schools in your area to see if this is an option. This coursework will, of course, be part of your admissions portfolio as part of your transcript, since you are required to release all grades in all courses taken at a post-high-school level as part of your American Medical

Colleges Application Service (AMCAS) application. This may be a benefit as well—doing well in these courses can help boost your nonscience and overall (Biology, Physics, Chemistry, and Math (BPCM) and nonscience courses) GPAs.

IMPORTANT POINT

If you choose to learn biochemistry, psychology, and sociology at a local institution, recognize that the style of the questions and what that particular professor or school deems important may vary from what is seen on MCAT 2015. This is often evident with biochemistry. While courses may place an undue amount of focus on memorizing intermediates in the various metabolic processes in the body, MCAT 2015 will be testing biochemistry more conceptually and as "big picture" questions.

MED SCHOOL INSIGHT

In medical school, like on the MCAT, biochemistry is usually taught with more focus toward the regulation (and dysregulation) of a metabolic pathway, rather than memorizing intermediates and enzymes. For example, it's less important to know that δ-aminolevulinic acid dehydratase converts δ-aminolevulinic acid into porphobilinogen during heme synthesis (what a mouthful!). It's more important to recognize that when this enzyme is inactivated, such as by lead, that heme—a necessary component of hemoglobin in red blood cells—cannot be made and the patient may present with anemia (low hemoglobin in the blood).

- **Massive open online courses (MOOCs)**—A relatively new contributor to the education scene, MOOCs are open-access, free-of-charge courses offered online. Many MOOCs are run by universities, whose professors essentially move their lectures online. Depending on the school, these lectures may be prerecorded (and, thus, viewable at any time and in any order) or may stick with a course schedule for the corresponding course offered within their school. Other MOOCs are developed by independent companies, and therefore may not be held to the same rigorous level of quality as courses within a school. However, the affordability and flexibility of MOOCs make them a great option if you're viewing your study of biochemistry, psychology, and sociology as a "supplement" to everything else you're doing day-to-day. MOOCs do not require formal registration and are free to anyone with an internet connection. Their focus on maintaining interactivity, even in this online environment, often makes these courses fun and memorable. Gamification—or turning educational progress into a game through points, badges, or awards as you advance from "level" to "level" (or skill to skill)—can make the learning process entertaining. However, recognize that MOOCs usually do not have formal assessment tools built into them. Their quality (and accuracy) can vary, depending on the provider of the course. And MOOCs are not the equivalent of test prep, since they do not focus on these subjects the way they'll be tested on MCAT 2015.

- **Review books**—We're leaving the Kaplan review books out of this category, since they were covered in the first bullet point; instead, let's turn our attention to some of the other common book series developed for medical and undergraduate review. You've seen these in bookstores and online—short books that offer a "crash course" in the content of a particular subject. These books can be very helpful in boiling down the information into a quick, convenient read. But notice that this is *boiling*, not *distilling*: Yes, these books do reduce the volume of information into a more manageable amount, but they do not always separate the high-yield information from the minutiae. Like many of the other study resources previously mentioned, review books may cast too wide a net for what's covered in MCAT 2015. Therefore, if you choose to study predominantly through review books, make sure to cross-reference what you're learning with what's listed in the *Preview Guide for the MCAT²⁰¹⁵ Exam* to make sure you're covering everything you need and not getting too entrenched in material that's *not* considered "fair game" for Test Day. To their credit, many review books have a number of review questions at the end, which may include critical thinking, short-answer, and multiple-choice formats. While these are not explicitly written in MCAT 2015 style and are usually unassociated with a passage, they do give you the opportunity to make sure you comprehend the content and are able to apply it in new scenarios.

CHAPTER LINK/FIND MORE ONLINE

In addition to checking the *Preview Guide for the MCAT²⁰¹⁵ Exam* online for content lists of what you're expected to know for the new exam, check out Chapter 7 for a distilled list of the new content being added to MCAT 2015.

- **Standard textbooks**—In the era before quality test prep courses, textbooks long-dominated the realm of self-study for tests like the MCAT. However, we now do not recommend textbooks for the purposes of learning the biochemistry, psychology, and sociology material you need to know for MCAT 2015. Textbooks cover way too much information that is *not* necessary for success on Test Day, are large and unwieldy study sources for a quick review of the material, and can often be expensive. While textbooks could help serve as a supplement to the other study strategies you're employing— especially for points of clarification, increased depth, or practice problems—they should not be the primary resource you're using. Plus, that's an awful lot to read when you still have eight other courses' worth of material to review before Test Day.

GAUGING YOUR STUDY MATERIALS

In this section, we provide three critical thinking questions for each of the new subjects on MCAT 2015: biochemistry, psychology, and sociology. The answers provided are reflective of the depth to which you should understand and be able to apply the material on Test Day and should be used as a gauge to determine if your study materials are adequate and appropriate for MCAT 2015. The questions are relatively narrow, and certainly do not encompass all of the content you need for Test Day, but rather reflect a small sample of the topics your resources should cover.

Biochemistry

How does the body determine when to *use* glucose (glycolysis) versus *create* glucose (gluconeogenesis); what are the most important targets to switch from one process to the other?

In general, metabolism is regulated by three main mechanisms: hormonal (the levels of insulin and glucagon, as well as a few other regulatory hormones like cortisol, epinephrine/norepinephrine, and growth hormone), energetic (the relative amounts of ATP, ADP, and AMP) and feedback (predominantly negative feedback from products of a given metabolic pathway). In the case of glycolysis, the body should be well-fed and in need of energy (high insulin, low ATP). In the case of gluconeogenesis, the body should have low blood glucose but be able to obtain enough energy from other fuels to drive this process (high glucagon, high ATP). Most of the reactions in glycolysis and gluconeogenesis are the same—just flowing in opposite directions. However, the most highly regulated targets necessarily are the rate-limiting steps in each process, since this would determine which process can be active at any given time.

When you take a daily multivitamin, what are all of those vitamins and minerals for?

Multivitamins are made up of a number of organic compounds (vitamins) and inorganic ions or metals (minerals). Vitamins can also be referred to as coenzymes, and minerals as cofactors. In both cases, these compounds help enzymes to accomplish the single reaction they catalyze (enzyme specificity) by providing energy, which causes a conformational shift in the enzyme and promotes its activity. Minerals that are very tightly bound to an enzyme, and thus are necessary for its function, are referred to as prosthetic groups. You are not responsible for knowing every vitamin and mineral, and the reactions in which they participate, for MCAT 2015; however, you should know conceptually what the overall functions are for vitamins and minerals as a group.

Below is a double reciprocal (Lineweaver-Burk) plot of a hypothetical enzyme catalyzing a reaction in a dish. What would happen to this line if a noncompetitive inhibitor were added to the dish?

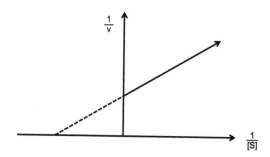

Double reciprocal or Lineweaver-Burk plots are a staple of enzymology in biochemistry. Note that the graph has $1/v$ for its y-axis (v representing the speed of the reaction) and $1/[S]$ for its x-axis ([S] representing the concentration of the substrate). You should be familiar with two important points in this graph: the x-intercept represents $-1/K_m$, where K_m is the Michaelis-Menten constant that reflects the affinity of the enzyme for its substrate;

on the other hand, the y-intercept represents v_{max}, the maximal speed of the reaction. When one adds a noncompetitive inhibitor to the reaction, the inhibitor will cause some copies of the enzyme to become inactive and unable to catalyze the reaction. Therefore, v_{max} decreases (or $1/v_{max}$ increases). The y-intercept has thus increased. The noncompetitive inhibitor does not impact the affinity of the remaining copies of the enzyme for their substrate, so the x-intercept should not change. The new line would look something like this:

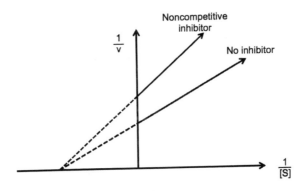

One could also determine what a Lineweaver-Burk plot would look like for the same situation, but with a competitive inhibitor added instead. We'll leave the full derivation out, but one would expect the line to have the same y-intercept, but with a less negative x-intercept (that is, the x-intercept moves to the right, closer to zero).

Psychology

What is the difference between positive and negative reinforcement, punishment, and extinction?

All of these terms are associated with operant conditioning, in which the consequence of a given behavior serves to continue that behavior (positive and negative reinforcement) or stop that behavior (punishment and extinction). Sometimes, these four behaviors are plotted in a graphic form:

		Stimulus	
		Added	Removed
Behavior	Continues	Positive reinforcement	Negative reinforcement
	Stops	Punishment	Extinction

- Positive reinforcement is like a "reward" system. A stimulus is added, and, as a result, the behavior continues. For example, employees are given a raise (stimulus) to continue working hard (behavior).

- Negative reinforcement occurs when the removal of a stimulus promotes a given behavior. For example, a teenage boy may learn that his parents will stop nagging him (stimulus) when he cleans his room (behavior). Negative reinforcement is *not* the same thing as punishment, although we often incorrectly use these terms interchangeably in everyday speech.

- Punishment occurs when the addition of a stimulus stops a behavior from occurring. For example, a thief may be arrested and charged (stimulus) to discourage him or her from stealing again (behavior).

- Extinction occurs when the removal of a stimulus stops a behavior from occurring. For example, a parent may ignore or stop paying attention to a toddler (stimulus) when he or she throws a temper tantrum (behavior).

Many diseases can result from an imbalance of neurotransmitters, like dopamine in the brain. Describe a disease caused by an excess of dopamine and a disease caused by a deficit of dopamine. Why is knowing this relationship important?

Psychotic disorders, the most important of which for MCAT 2015 is schizophrenia, are associated with an excess of dopamine in a number of pathways in the brain. The main features of schizophrenia include delusions (fixed, false beliefs that do not match one's society), auditory hallucinations (hearing voices), abnormal and disorganized thinking and language patterns, unusual movements, and an inability to take care of oneself.

Parkinson's disease is caused by the death of dopamine-releasing neurons, causing a decrease in the overall amount of dopamine in the brain. The main features of Parkinson's disease include tremors (often called "pill-rolling" tremors), slow movement, shuffling while walking, and rigidity of the muscles. Dementia tends to show up as a late symptom.

It is important to recognize the relationship between these two diseases, because the treatments of one may cause the other. For example, the dopamine-blocking medications used in schizophrenia can cause "parkinsonism" as a side effect. On the other hand, the dopamine-enhancing medications used in Parkinson's disease can cause psychosis as a side effect.

What are some of the main brainwave features of each sleep stage?

When describing sleep stages, we should keep in mind our knowledge of the normal sleep cycle with the different electroencephalographic (EEG) waveforms that accompany normal sleep patterns.

- **Non-rapid Eye Movement (NREM) Sleep:**
    - **Stage 1** (lightest sleep)—theta waves on EEG; accounts for 5% of sleep.
    - **Stage 2** (light sleep)—sleep spindles and K-complexes on EEG; accounts for 45% of sleep.

- ○ **Stage 3 and 4** (deep sleep)—slow (delta) waves on EEG; accounts for 25% of sleep. Also called slow-wave sleep (SWS), this is the most restful sleep during the night and is the first type of sleep "made up" when an individual has sleep deprivation.
- **Rapid Eye Movement (REM) Sleep:** sawtooth waves on EEG and rapid eye movement, paralysis (loss of muscle tone), nighttime erections (in males); accounts for 25% of sleep. REM sleep is reached only after the brain cycles through the four NREM stages at the beginning of the night. Later during the night, REM sleep alternates with SWS.
- **Awake:** alpha and beta waves on EEG.

Sociology

What do ethnocentrism and cultural relativism share in common? What is different between these two concepts?

Ethnocentrism is the idea that one's culture is superior to all other cultures. This often plays out at the individual level by a person defining those people that are "in-group" (belonging to this same social group) versus "out-group" (not belonging to this same social group, or belonging to a different social group). This sense of superiority, in its most extreme form, can lead to discrimination and mistreatment.

Cultural relativism is the perception of another culture as different from one's own, but with the recognition that the cultural values, mores, and rules of a society fit that society itself. In other words, while one group may follow a given set of rules (say, the dietary rules of kashrut or halal), that group does not perceive those rules as superior to other cultures'—just different.

In both cases—ethnocentrism and cultural relativism—an individual perceives another group to which he or she does not belong. However, it is the *reaction* to that other group that reflects which paradigm is being used.

Some individuals may be stigmatized for their illness, while others are not. Why is this?

Stigma, in sociology, is defined as the extreme disapproval of an individual by other members of a society based on a particular social characteristic that differentiates the individual from society at large. When considering disease, one of the major factors that promotes stigmatization is responsibility. If an individual is perceived to be responsible for his or her illness, he or she can be stigmatized because of it. Typically, people with sexually transmitted infections (STIs), mental illness, addiction, or developmental disabilities suffer from such stigma because they are thought to be at fault for being sick—whether or not this is actually true. Similarly, if a person does not seek treatment for one of these conditions, he or she can also be stigmatized for not treating something that is within his or her control to treat. For example, an alcoholic going through alcohol withdrawal would likely suffer stigma for this condition because he or she is held responsible for causing this illness.

Medicine and other related fields are still working to bring men and women on equal ground with respect to number of available positions for residency graduates and equal wages. More generally, what are some causes of the wage gap between genders in the U.S.?

There is a significant wage gap between men and women. One reason is that women may confront a "glass ceiling," which consists of artificial barriers to their promotion within an organization. One example of an artificial barrier is the stereotype that ambitious women are not feminine enough. Another reason why the wage gap exists is that there is significant occupational sex segregation, and jobs where women cluster are generally paid less than jobs where men dominate. For example, elementary school teachers (a female-dominated occupation) are paid less than firefighters (a male-dominated occupation). Additionally, women are penalized in the form of lower wages each time they exit the labor force to have or care for a child. Other factors certainly exist, as well.

Now that we've seen the content that MCAT 2015 will test, and how to prepare yourself for that material, let's take a look at *how* MCAT 2015 will be asking questions. What thinking skills will each question focus on?

CHAPTER 11

The Skills That MCAT 2015 Will Test

Success on any standardized exam requires some amount of outside knowledge and some amount of performance skills. The current MCAT, for example, tests physics, chemistry, and biology, but that's not all; it also tests your ability to make accurate calculations, infer an author's opinion based on his or her tone, and mentally perform under tight time constraints. This separation between the outside knowledge demanded by an exam, and the test-taking skills it measures, is an important distinction for test takers to understand, as these different domains require different types of studying and practice.

Fortunately, the AAMC has been fairly explicit about what skills they will expect you to demonstrate on MCAT 2015. In fact, the *Preview Guide for the MCAT²⁰¹⁵ Exam* explains that the science sections and the CARS section will each demand different skill sets; the AAMC calls these sets "Scientific Inquiry and Reasoning Skills" and "CARS Skills," respectively. In this chapter, we'll first dive into each of the four science skills, and then into each of the three CARS skills. For every skill, we'll examine a longer list of objectives within the skill, we'll explain what the skill means in a general sense, and then we'll see some sample question stems that would test the skill.

TEST DAY TIP

It's easy enough to learn what skills will be tested on the MCAT 2015, but it's another thing altogether to train for and master these skills for Test Day. Ultimately, that training requires a well-defined study plan that assesses your performance on each skill, corrects your deficiencies, and gives you plenty of test-like practice and good coaching—the last of which is a process you'll have to start closer to Test Day itself. For a short introduction on how to formally prepare yourself for the exam, check out Chapters 9 and 10 of this book.

SCIENTIFIC INQUIRY AND REASONING SKILLS

The AAMC has defined four Scientific Inquiry and Reasoning Skills (or just "MCAT Science Skills") that will be tested on the Chem/Phys, Bio/Biochem, and Psych/Soc sections of the MCAT 2015. While the rates at which these skills will be tested on the science sections have not yet been confirmed by the AAMC, it's fair to assume that they will be tested in roughly equal amounts, with Skills 1 and 2 tested slightly more often than Skills 3 and 4. But, however the exact skill frequencies work out between now and the spring of 2015, it's certain that mastering all of them will be vital to scoring well on the science sections.

The four science skills are:

1. Science Knowledge
2. Scientific Reasoning and Problem Solving
3. Experimental and Research Design
4. Data and Statistical Analysis

Let's see how each one breaks down into more specific Test Day behaviors.

MCAT FACTS

These Science Skill names are slightly shorter (and, we hope, clearer) than the exact names used by the AAMC in the *Preview Guide to the MCAT2015 Exam*. The bullet points of specific behaviors beneath each skill are, however, directly in line with what has been published by the testmaker.

Skill 1: Science Knowledge

This is probably the least surprising of the four skills; the testing of science knowledge is, after all, one of the signature qualities of the MCAT. Skill 1 questions will require you to:

- Recognize correct scientific principles
- Identify the relationships among closely-related concepts
- Identify the relationships between different representations of concepts (verbal, symbolic, graphic)
- Identify examples of observations that illustrate scientific principles
- Use mathematical equations to solve problems

Another way to think of Skill 1 questions is as "one-step" problems. The single step is either to realize which scientific concept the question stem is hinting at, or to take the concept stated in the question stem and identify which answer choice is an accurate application of it. We expect that Skill 1 will be particularly prominent among discrete questions (those not associated with a passage), but regardless of where they are found, these questions will be your opportunity for gaining the quickest points on Test Day—if you know the science concept attached to the question, then that's it!

Here are some sample Skill 1 question stems:

How would a proponent of the James-Lange theory of emotion interpret the findings of the study cited the passage?

Which of the following most accurately describes the function of FSH in the human female menstrual cycle?

If the products of Reaction 1 and Reaction 2 were combined in solution, the resulting reaction would form:

Ionic bonds are maintained by which of the following forces?

Skill 2: Scientific Reasoning and Problem Solving

The MCAT 2015 science sections will, of course, move beyond testing straightforward science knowledge; Skill 2 questions are the most common way in which it will do so. Skill 2 questions will require you to:

- Reason about scientific principles, theories, and models
- Analyze and evaluate scientific explanations and predictions
- Evaluate arguments about causes and consequences
- Bring together theory, observations, and evidence to draw conclusions
- Recognize scientific findings that challenge or invalidate a scientific theory or model
- Determine and use scientific formulas to solve problems

Just as Skill 1 questions can be thought of as "one-step" problems, many Skill 2 questions will be "two-step" problems, and more difficult Skill 2 questions may require three or more steps. These questions can require a wide spectrum of reasoning skills, including integration of multiple facts from a passage, combination of multiple science content areas, and prediction of an experiment's results. Skill 2 questions also tend to ask about science content without actually mentioning it by name; for example, a question might describe the results of one experiment and ask you to predict the results of a second experiment without actually telling you what underlying scientific principles are at work—part of the question's difficulty will be figuring out which principles to apply in order to get the correct answer.

Here are some sample Skill 2 question stems:

> Which of the following experimental conditions would most likely yield results similar to those in Figure 2?

> All of the following conclusions are supported by the information in the passage EXCEPT:

> The most likely cause of the anomalous results found by the experimenter is:

> An impact to a man's chest quickly reduces the volume of one of his lungs to 70% of its initial value, while not allowing any air to escape from the man's mouth. By what percentage is the force of outward air pressure increased on a 2 cm^2 portion of the inner surface of the compressed lung?

Skill 3: Experimental and Research Design

The MCAT has always tested knowledge of experimental and research design in a marginal capacity, but the new exam will place increased emphasis on this skill, thereby making it a large portion of your Test Day experience. Skill 3 questions will require you to:

- Identify the role of theory, past findings, and observations in scientific questioning
- Identify testable research questions and hypotheses
- Distinguish between samples and populations and distinguish results that support generalizations about populations
- Identify independent and dependent variables
- Reason about the features of research studies that suggest associations between variables or causal relationships between them (e.g., temporality, random assignment)

- Identify conclusions that are supported by research results
- Determine the implications of results for real-world situations
- Reason about ethical issues in scientific research

Over the years, the AAMC has received input from medical schools to require more "practical research skills" of MCAT test takers, and Skill 3 questions are the response to these demands. This skill is unique in that the outside knowledge you need to answer Skill 3 questions is not taught in any one undergraduate course; instead, the research design principles needed to answer these questions are learned gradually throughout your science classes, and especially through any laboratory work you have completed. A Research Methods in Psychology course (a 100- or 200-level course offered at most colleges and universities) will also be a particularly good source for facts relevant to Skill 3, since we anticipate that the most in-depth questions on this skill will appear on the new Psych/Soc section of the exam.

TEST DAY TIP

Since Skill 3 knowledge is so dispersed among undergraduate courses, it will be easy to miss some of these principles when they are discussed in your prerequisite college courses. As a result, specialized MCAT preparation courses will be one of the best resources for highlighting the principles of experimental and research design that you will see on the new exam.

Here are some sample Skill 3 question stems:

What is the dependent variable in the study described in the passage?

The major flaw in the method used to measure disease susceptibility in Experiment 1 is:

Which of the following procedures is most important for the experimenters to follow in order for their study to maintain a proper, randomized sample of research subjects?

A researcher would like to test the hypothesis that individuals who move to an urban area during adulthood are more likely to own a car than those who have lived in an urban area since birth. Which of the following studies would best test this hypothesis?

Skill 4: Data and Statistical Analysis

Lastly, the science sections of the MCAT 2015 will test your ability to analyze the visual and numerical results of experiments and studies. Skill 4 questions will require you to:

- Use, analyze, and interpret data in figures, graphs, and tables
- Evaluate whether representations make sense for particular scientific observations and data
- Use measures of central tendency (mean, median, and mode) and measures of dispersion (range, inter-quartile range, and standard deviation) to describe data
- Reason about random and systematic error
- Reason about statistical significance and uncertainty (interpreting statistical significance levels, interpreting a confidence interval)
- Use data to explain relationships between variables or make predictions
- Use data to answer research questions and draw conclusions

Skill 4, like Skill 3, has always been tested on the MCAT, albeit in a limited capacity. However, it is becoming a larger share of MCAT 2015. This is because physicians and researchers do, after all, spend much of their time examining the results of their own studies and the studies of others, and it's very important for them to make legitimate conclusions and sound judgments based on that data. MCAT 2015 will test Skill 4 on all three science sections, and it will do so with graphical representations of data (charts and bar graphs) as well as numerical ones (tables, lists, and results summarized in sentence or paragraph form).

Here are some sample Skill 4 question stems:

> According to the information in the passage, there is an inverse correlation between:

> What conclusion is best supported by the findings displayed in Figure 2?

> A medical test for a rare type of heavy metal poisoning returns a positive result for 98% of affected individuals and 13% of unaffected individuals. Which of the following type of error is most prevalent in this test?

> If a fourth trial of Experiment 1 was run and yielded a result of 54% compliance, which of the following would be true?

Science Skills Summary

Discussing the skills to be tested on the science sections of the MCAT 2015 is a daunting prospect, given that the very nature of the skills tends to make the conversation rather abstract. Nevertheless, with enough practice, you'll be able to identify each of the four skills quickly, and you'll also be able to apply the proper strategies to solve those problems on Test Day. If you need a quick reference to remind you of the four Science Skills, these guidelines may help:

Skill 1 (Science Knowledge) questions ask:

> "Do you remember this science content?"

Skill 2 (Scientific Reasoning and Problem Solving) questions ask:

> "Do you remember this science content? And if you do, could you please apply it to this novel situation?"

> OR

> "Could you answer this question that cleverly combines multiple content areas at the same time?"

Skill 3 (Experimental and Research Design) questions ask:

"Let's forget about the science content for a while. Could you give some insight into the experimental or research methods involved in this situation?"

Skill 4 (Data and Statistical Analysis) questions ask:

"Let's forget about the science content for a while. Could you accurately read some graphs and tables for a moment? Maybe you could make some conclusions or extrapolations based on the information presented?"

IMPORTANT POINT

Even though the AAMC has taken time and effort to explicitly define each of these Science Skills, you should *not* assume that these skills will only be tested one at a time. Each question will have a "primary" skill to test that is more prominent than any of the others, but you will also see some blending of skills on the exam. For instance, some questions that primarily test data interpretation (Skill 4) may also require supplementary knowledge of research design (Skill 3) or scientific formulas (Skill 2).

CARS SKILLS

The Critical Analysis and Reasoning Skills (CARS) section of MCAT 2015 will test three discrete families of textual reasoning skills; each of these families will require a higher level of reasoning than the last. Those three skills are:

1. Comprehension (approximately 30% of CARS questions)
2. Reasoning Within the Text (approximately 30% of CARS questions)
3. Reasoning Beyond the Text (approximately 40% of CARS questions)

MCAT FACTS

The percentages assigned to each question type come directly from the AAMC's *Preview Guide for the MCAT2015 Exam*.

These three skills will be tested through multiple humanities- and social science-themed passages, with 5 to 7 questions per passage. Let's take a more in-depth look into these three skills.

IMPORTANT POINT

Even though this organization of CARS skills is new for MCAT 2015, we anticipate that MCAT 2015 will test all of the same major question types and styles of reasoning that the current MCAT does. So even though this taxonomy may look new if you're already familiar with the Verbal Reasoning section of the current MCAT, rest assured that the two sections will still be quite similar.

Comprehension

Questions in this skill will ask for basic facts and inferences about the passage; the questions themselves will be similar to those seen on reading comprehension sections of other standardized exams like the SAT and ACT. This admittedly covers a wide range of potential question types, but the correct answer to all Comprehension questions will follow from a basic understanding of the passage and the point of view of its author (and occasionally that of other main characters in the passage). A few Comprehension questions will also depend on finding the right detail in the passage, but the MCAT generally dislikes these "treasure hunt" questions, so we don't expect MCAT 2015 to have many of them.

Here are some sample Comprehension question stems:

Based on the information in the second paragraph, which of the following is the most accurate summary of the opinion held by Schubert's critics?

The author's primary purpose in this passage is:

Which of the following is implied by the author's discussion of the effect of socioeconomic status on social mobility?

The word "obscure" (paragraph 3), when used in reference to the historian's actions, most nearly means:

In putting forth his argument in the passage, the author assumes which of the following to be true?

According to the passage, which of the following is true about literary reviews in the 1920s?

FIND MORE ONLINE

The AAMC has not released point-by-point lists of question types for the CARS section like they have for the four Science Skills. We do suspect, though, that the question-type breakdown will be extremely similar—possibly even identical—to the list of Verbal Reasoning Cognitive Skills being used for the current MCAT. (To understand the list in terms of MCAT 2015 skills, "Evaluation" can be equated with "Reasoning Within the Text" and both "Application" and "Incorporation" are contained within "Reasoning Beyond the Text.")

Reasoning Within the Text

While Comprehension questions will usually depend on interpreting a single piece of information in the passage or understanding the passage as a whole, Reasoning Within the Text questions will typically require you to bring together two disparate pieces of the passage, or to understand how a single detail fits into the purpose of the passage as a whole. In other words, questions in this skill often ask either "How do these two details relate to one another?" or "What role does this detail play in the passage as a whole?"

TEST DAY TIP

The relationship between Comprehension and Reasoning Within the Text is similar to the relationship between Skill 1 (Science Knowledge) and Skill 2 (Scientific Reasoning and Problem Solving) of the MCAT Science Skills. In each pairing, the first skill tests "one-step" questions, while the second tests "multistep" questions.

The CARS section of MCAT 2015 will also ask you to judge certain parts of the passage, or even judge the author. These questions, which fall under the Reasoning Within the Text skill, can ask you to identify authorial bias, evaluate the credibility of cited sources, determine the logical soundness of an argument, or search for relevant evidence in the passage to support a given conclusion.

Here are some sample Reasoning Within the Text question stems:

Which of the following facts is used in the passage as the most prominent piece of evidence in favor of the author's conclusions?

Based on the role it plays in the author's argument, *The Possessed* can be considered:

The argument of the scholars quoted in the third paragraph is vulnerable to which of the following criticisms?

Which of the following phrases, as used in the passage, is most suggestive that the author has a personal bias toward narrative records of history?

Reasoning Beyond the Text

The distinguishing factor of Reasoning Beyond the Text questions is right there in the title of the skill: the word "beyond." Questions that test this skill, which will make up a larger share of the CARS section than questions from either of the other two CARS skills, will always introduce a completely new situation that was not present in the passage itself; these questions will ask you to determine how one influences the other. The Reasoning Beyond the Text skill is further divided into two separate question types, depending on which concept—the passage or the new situation—is the influencer and which is being influenced.

Application questions will call out a principle or concept from the passage, and they will ask how that concept would inform or influence a newly presented situation. In other words, it asks you to *apply* the principles or patterns of the passage (such as the author's opinion) to new circumstances.

Incorporation questions will present some new, outside information as fact (either in the question stem or as answer choices), and they will ask you how that new information influences the passage or the arguments within it. Usually the result of *incorporating* this new information into the passage is either a strengthening or a weakening of the arguments in the passage.

Here are some sample Reasoning Beyond the Text question stems:

Based on the information in the passage, with which of the following statements about literary criticism is the author most likely to agree? (Application)

Which of the following is the best example of a "virtuous rebellion," as it is defined in the passage? (Application)

Suppose Jane Austen had written in a letter to her sister, "My strongest characters were those forced by circumstance to confront basic questions about the society in which they lived." What relevance would this have to the passage? (Incorporation)

Which of the following sentences, if added to the end of the passage, would most WEAKEN the author's conclusions in the last paragraph? (Incorporation)

CARS Skills Summary

Through the Comprehension skill, the CARS section of MCAT 2015 will test many of the reading skills you have been building since grade school, albeit in the context of very challenging, doctorate-level passages. But through the two other skills (Reasoning Within the Text and Reasoning Beyond the Text), MCAT 2015 will demand that you understand the deep structure of passages and the arguments within them at a very advanced level. And, of course, all of this will be tested under very tight timing restrictions: only 90 seconds per question, and that doesn't even include the time spent reading the passages.

TEST DAY TIP

The CARS section of MCAT 2015 will be very challenging—probably the most challenging reading test you've ever taken. We've made this point before, but that's because it's so vital: To succeed on this section, you'll have to practice extensive amounts of high-level reading and CARS section practice. There's just no other way to succeed on this material under MCAT-level timing and stamina pressures.

Here's a quick reference guide to the three CARS skills:

Comprehension questions ask:

"Did you understand the passage and its main ideas?"

OR

"What does the passage have to say about this particular detail?"

Reasoning Within the Text questions ask:

"What's the logical relationship between these two ideas from the passage?"

OR

"What role does this part of the passage play in the author's argument?"

OR

"How well-argued is the author's thesis?"

Reasoning Beyond the Text questions ask:

"How does this principle from the passage apply to this new situation?" (Application)
OR
"How does this new piece of information influence the arguments in the passage?" (Incorporation)

Sample Questions and Test-taking Strategies

In this chapter, you'll find a full representative passage from each section, along with its associated questions and detailed explanations. Use the information in this chapter not only to analyze how you're performing with the content and critical thinking that MCAT 2015 will demand, but also to pick up some strategies you can use on Test Day.

CRITICAL ANALYSIS AND REASONING SKILLS (CARS)

Do you remember the last time you were given a required reading list? You probably sighed and tried to figure out how long it would take you to read all of those books. Well, beware that there will be required reading on MCAT 2015, too, but the good news is that you know exactly how long it will take—90 minutes—and, luckily, you don't have to write a research paper or an analysis essay at the end. All you have to do is answer some questions correctly after reading.

Fundamentally, the CARS section of MCAT 2015 requires you to do three things: read critically, think, and analyze. Thus, the CARS section is the section on MCAT 2015 that will be the most responsive to strategy practice. This means you can do well on the CARS section, despite not having specific facts or science to fall back on.

Let's take a look at a sample passage, paragraph by paragraph, to see how to best think through passages on the new CARS section.

Passage I (Questions 1–7)

Read the following passage, and then answer the questions.

Paragraph 1

According to our traditional understanding of responsibility, we are primarily responsible for our "voluntary" actions, the things we do, and (at most) only indirectly responsible for the things that happen to us. It is held, for instance, that "I can't help" the surge of anger, say, that I feel when objects in the environment present themselves to my senses in certain ways. When we look inside ourselves with the goal of sorting our mental events into these two morally important categories, something peculiar happens. Events near the input and output "peripheries" fall unproblematically into place. Thus, feeling pain in my foot and seeing the desk are clearly not acts "in my control," but things that happen to me as a result of impingements from the world. And moving my finger or saying these words are obviously things that I do—voluntary actions par excellence.

This is a long and dense paragraph, so don't be surprised if you're anxious or confused already. Let's just break this paragraph down so we can understand it better. It starts off with a comparison of "voluntary" actions and actions that happen to us. To make the discussion easier, let's call the latter type of action "involuntary." In the next sentence, we see the key words "for instance" which means that an example is coming. Since examples simply depict the same train of thought, we can just skim this sentence. On the other hand, the third sentence reveals the author's primary purpose (a helpful thing to find on Test Day!): Actions are being sorted into either the voluntary category or the involuntary category. We also discover in this third sentence that something out of the ordinary happens. It is important to keep this "peculiar" event in mind as you finish reading the paragraph. What you find is that the author almost seems to forget about this "peculiar" statement. The rest of the paragraph simply describes events in the "input and output peripheries" which are easy to sort into voluntary and involuntary actions. It is at this point that you can anticipate what is coming next, and this will aid in your comprehension of the passage so far. If events in the "input and output peripheries" are easy to sort, but then something "peculiar" happens, other events must be oddly *not* easy to sort. And this is what we see in the next paragraph.

Paragraph 2

But as we move away from those peripheries toward the presumptive center, the events we try to examine exhibit a strange flickering back and forth. It no longer seems so clear that perception is a passive matter. Do I not voluntarily contribute something to my perception, even to my recognition or "acceptance" of the desk as a desk? For after all, can I not suspend judgment in the face of any perceptual presentation, and withhold conviction? And on the other side of the center, when we look more closely at action, is my voluntary act really moving my finger, or is it more properly trying to move my finger? A familiar [thought experiment] about someone willing actions while totally paralyzed attests that I am not in control of all the conditions in the world that are necessary for my finger actually to move.

We see another dense paragraph here, but this time we were prepared. We anticipated that the author was most likely going to discuss actions that are harder to categorize than simply voluntary or involuntary, and he or she does just that. Thus, you can skim this paragraph, because you've got the main point already; most of the rest of the paragraph is just examples. The only issue now is that the author presents two seemingly contradictory points toward the end of the paragraph; so, we can anticipate a resolution in the next paragraph.

Paragraph 3

Faced with our inability to "see" (by "introspection") where the center or source of our free actions is, and loath to abandon our conviction that we really do things (for which we are responsible), we exploit the cognitive vacuum by filling it with a rather magical and mysterious entity, the unmoved mover, the active self.

Yes, this entire paragraph is one long and convoluted sentence. But that's okay! Remember, you're not supposed to read the passages in the CARS section like you would read a textbook—trying to understand everything all the time. If you can get the gist here, you will have all you need to answer the questions. Actually, this intense sentence/paragraph actually sets us up nicely to find the gist because it all leads to describing the last few words: the active self. Remember, this paragraph was supposed to contain our resolution, so now we know that the "active self" is our resolution. Since that is all we need for this paragraph, we can move on to the next paragraph.

Paragraph 4

This theoretical leap is nowhere more evident than in our reaction to our failures of "willpower." "I'm going to get out of bed and get to work right now!" I say to myself, and go right on lying in bed. Did I or did I not just make a decision to get up? Can't I tell when I've really made a decision? Perhaps I just seem to myself to have made a decision. Once we recognize that our conscious access to our own decisions is problematic, we may go on to note how many of the important turning points in our lives were unaccompanied, so far as retrospective memory of conscious experience goes, by conscious decisions. "I have decided to take the job," one says. And very clearly one takes oneself to be reporting on something one had done recently, but reminiscence shows only that yesterday one was undecided, and today one is no longer undecided; at some moment in the interval the decision must have happened, without fanfare. Where did it happen? At Central Headquarters, of course.

Again, a long paragraph, but luckily it is written in a slightly easier reading style than the previous paragraphs. The examples that you hopefully skimmed through show a scope shift from discussing general actions to discussing decisions specifically. Now, instead of discussing simply voluntary versus involuntary actions, the author is talking about categorizing decisions and whether we consciously remember making them or not. Once again, the active self is alluded to here (Central Headquarters) as the thing that resolves this conflict. And with that, we tackle the final paragraph.

Paragraph 5

But such a deduction reveals that we are building a psychological theory of "decision" by idealizing and extending our actual practice, by inserting decisions where theory demands them, not where we have any firsthand experience of them. I must have made a decision, one reasons, since I see that I have definitely made up my mind, and hadn't made up my mind yesterday. The mysterious inner sanctum of the central agent begins to take on a life of its own.

This paragraph is exciting because the active self is finally explained in some detail. The author discusses "idealizing and extending our actual practice." This convoluted phrase describes what some morally disinclined people might do on their medical school applications—in short, it is "embellishing what one actually does." For example, one could say that a visit to the doctor for treatment of a virus counted as a "significant and ongoing career-shadowing experience." Of course, you would never do this, but the example helps us to understand the author's main point. That is, we often can't resolve whether our actions or decisions are the ones we consciously wanted, so we make up a mysterious being in our minds that must be acting or deciding for us.

So you don't lose track of all the great reasoning you do when reading passages in the CARS section, it is good to jot down very brief notes while reading each paragraph—we call these passage maps. Here is an example of what you could write for this passage:

Paragraph 1: Old view of voluntary and involuntary actions.

Paragraph 2: Overlap of voluntary and involuntary actions.

Paragraph 3: The active self resolves this overlap we feel.

Paragraph 4: Shift to decisions, can't remember making some of them.

Paragraph 5: The inner sanctum is where decisions are made and we can't always sense it.

Topic: Voluntary/involuntary actions and decisions.

Scope: Classifying actions and remembering decisions.

Purpose: To argue that we can't classify all acts nor remember all decisions.

Armed with your notes and critical reading of the passage, you're now ready to tackle the questions associated with this passage. Let's start off slowly, taking the first question apart to see the thought process needed to score points.

Questions

Question 1

The passage's central thesis is that:

On Test Day, there will be answers following each question. However, to properly orient your thinking, we will hold off on looking at the answer choices and just work through the question. "Central thesis" questions like this one are testing a skill the AAMC calls Foundations of Comprehension, specifically the "overall meaning" component. Luckily, we already summarized the overall meaning in our notes. A quick reread of the Topic, Scope, and Purpose can give us a good idea of about what our answer should be. Now that we have predicted what the answer should look like, we can attempt to find it in the choices.

    A.   One should not be held responsible for actions over which one exerts no control.

    B.   Our sense that we can act voluntarily is an illusion.

    C.   Decisions are the instants in which we exercise our volition to the fullest.

    D.   Many actions cannot be classified precisely as either voluntary or involuntary.

Well, **answer choice (D)** matches our notes almost perfectly! This is the correct answer, and it is very exciting because we successfully dissected the passage and question. The other choices might have been tempting if you hadn't used the notes to decide what the answer was ahead of time. Nevertheless, you did know what to look for, and therefore, you weren't tricked by the distractor choices. Choice (A) reflects paragraph 1's traditional view. Choice (B) distorts what the author says: Paragraph 1 says some actions are "unproblematically" voluntary. Finally, choice (C) contradicts the author: Paragraphs 4 and 5 tell us that some decisions never happened.

Now, note that these overall meaning questions are fairly easy, so you won't see many of them on the CARS section. You might see a few detail questions, though, like the one that follows.

Question 2

According to the passage, if an individual has made a decision in the past, it:

Again, we want to think about this question before reading the answer choices and possibly falling for a cleverly worded distractor choice. Our notes can help us quickly find the paragraph(s) where this detail is found. It looks like the question is referring to paragraphs 4 and 5. The gist of those paragraphs is that we aren't sure when we make some decisions, so we invent decisions retroactively. With that choice in mind, take a look at the answer choices:

TEST DAY TIP

The more vague the prediction, the more closely you should read the choices.

A. automatically follows that the individual must assume full responsibility.
B. is sufficient proof that the individual possesses free will.
C. often cannot be ascertained how the individual knows he made the decision.
D. may not seem to the individual that there was any decision made at all.

In this question, our prediction isn't reflected word-for-word in an answer choice, but **answer choice (C)** is close. This choice is the correct answer. Once again, you can see that coming up with a good framework of what the answer should be really helps avoid picking those incorrect answers. Choice (A) is an application of the traditional view. Choice (B) isn't part of the passage, although it may sound feasible. Finally, choice (D) distorts information given in paragraphs 4 and 5; the point there is that individuals do believe decisions were made.

Global and detail questions are the easiest types of questions you will see in the CARS section. Let's increase the difficulty level with a deduction question next.

Question 3

Which of the following is a statement with which the author would most probably agree?

The author's opinions are found throughout the passage, so it will be hard to think of the exact answer before looking at the choices. But we do know that the choice has to reflect opinions that the author expressed, so go through the choices one at a time:

A.   People often exaggerate how much conscious thought went into their actions.
B.   A decision usually takes longer to make than one anticipates.
C.   Certain problems are better addressed through philosophical analysis than through science.
D.   More careful thought should go into decision making.

Answer choice (A) best matches the opinion expressed in the passage, specifically Paragraphs 4 and 5. The rest of the answer choices are classic types of incorrect answers that cover topics the author doesn't actually discuss, but may be tempting to a creative reader. Watch out for these types of answers on Test Day! The remaining answer choices are out of scope. Choice (B) isn't mentioned or compared. Choice (C) gives a contrast the author doesn't draw (see how helpful it is to note the contrasts that *are* set up by the author while you're reading). Finally, the author doesn't complain about rash decision making, as is reflected by choice (D).

Let's try another deduction question.

Question 4

> Judging from the context, the "unmoved mover" (paragraph 3) could best be described as:

This phrase in quotes is brought up in the passage where decision making is also being introduced (according to our notes). "The center or source of our free actions" is the definition of the phrase. So you can guess that the "unmoved mover" must be the part of us in charge of making decisions. Look for something like this in the choices.

> A. the divine being that many think guides one's actions.
> B. the inherent core of irrationality in human behavior.
> C. the part of the human psyche that governs decision making.
> D. the natural tendency to pursue one's self-interest.

Answer choice (C) is the only answer that doesn't go beyond what the author actually discusses in the passage. Deduction questions are usually in the medium range of difficulty in the CARS section, as are evaluation questions. Again, the remaining answer choices are out of scope. Choice (A) might be a choice based on common usage, but not based on the passage. Irrationality and self-interest are not discussed in the passage at all, so we can eliminate choices (B) and (D).

The next question is an example of an evaluation question where you're asked why a certain detail was included in the passage.

Question 5

> The author most probably cites "our failures of 'willpower'" (paragraph 4) in order to show that:

The author's point in this paragraph (again, from the notes we took) is to begin discussing decisions and the flaws in our understanding of them. The "failures of willpower" demonstrate that some decisions aren't even carried out. Thus, you can guess that the author references "failures of willpower" in order to show that we can seemingly make a conscious decision without acting on it. Look for this idea in the choices.

A. some people have more willpower than others.
B. one could possibly make a decision and yet not act on it.
C. some decisions are much more difficult to make than others.
D. the concept of willpower makes sense in theory but not in real life.

Answer choice (B) matches the prediction well. Again, the incorrect answer choices can sound great, but coming up with an idea of what to look for in the answer choices before reading them has really been paying off since it helps us avoid them. The remaining answer choices are again all out of scope. Choices (A) and (B) reflect comparisons that were never made in the passage. Choice (D) distorts the author's statements: The author says willpower doesn't apply sometimes.

Finally, let's try an application question, one of the most difficult questions types in the CARS section.

Question 6

Aristotle characterized a voluntary act as one whose source was "within the agent" and an involuntary act as "one of which the moving principle is outside." Based on the passage, the author would most likely respond to this by pointing out that:

Application questions like this one are there to test the AAMC Reasoning Beyond the Text skill. You must find a connection between the passage's ideas and new information. Aristotle's view is the traditional view, and the traditional view only works at extremes. Furthermore, in Paragraph 2, the author's view is that actions in the center are not so easily classified. Actions that fall in the middle cannot be classified strictly as voluntary or involuntary. Search for these ideas in the choices, being careful of distractors.

A. we are responsible only for our voluntary actions.
B. many actions contain elements of both categories.
C. there is no conscious judgment involved in an involuntary act.
D. the external moving principle is actually our own creation.

You should be looking at **answer choice (B)** because it is the only one that is close to our thought process after dissecting the question. Choices (A) and (C) both reflect the traditional view, not the author's. Finally, choice (D) distorts the author's view, since the moving principle the author talks about is internal.

Now you can move on to the final question—another tricky application question, this time with Roman numerals.

Question 7

Suppose that a person heats a kettle of water on a stove, takes it off the stove, and then accidentally spills some of the hot water on his or her skin. According to the passage, which of the following perceptions has a voluntary element?

I.   Perceiving that the hot stove caused the water to become hot
II. Perceiving that the kettle is made of steel
III. Perceiving the hot water as painful

To gain perspective on this question, refer to the example in the passage where author says we must contribute something to our understanding of a desk as a desk. This means that recognition of an item or process must have a voluntary element. Pain does not have this voluntary element, though. So, look through the statements and keep the choices that refer to something to which an individual must contribute understanding.

- I—has voluntary element (eliminate B)
- II—has voluntary element (eliminate A)
- III—no voluntary element (eliminate D)

A. I only
B. III only
C. I and II only
D. I, II, and III

Answer choice (C) is all that is left; it is correct. For III, remember that this perception has no voluntary element because we can't choose *not* to feel pain. One could choose not to *react* to pain, but he or she still can't stop the feeling. Also, one may not be able to feel pain due to certain body conditions, but body conditions are outside of voluntary control.

Congratulations on tackling your first test-like passage of the CARS section of MCAT 2015! As you can see, the CARS section puts great demands on your critical thinking and reasoning abilities, but with careful analysis and caution around the distractor choices, you can score as well as you did on this passage (100%) on many future CARS section passages.

CHEMICAL AND PHYSICAL FOUNDATIONS OF BIOLOGICAL SYSTEMS (CHEM/PHYS)

Now let's look at some example problems from the Chemical and Physical Foundations of Biological Systems, or Chem/Phys section, which is likely to be the first section you see when you take MCAT 2015. We'll review eight questions in all—six based on a passage and two discrete questions—and we'll give you some insight into how an MCAT expert would approach the questions. First, however, a warning: Some of these questions might seem very difficult, and the analysis may make you say, "How should I have known that?" But you'll see as you study for the exam that your own thoughts come closer and closer to how high-scorers think. And that's because you'll become a high-scorer yourself!

This is a passage that is just like what you'll see on Test Day in the Chem/Phys section. It tests principles of physics (electrostatics and circuits) and chemistry (ions) in the context of a biological system (the neuron). As you'll see, it also tests your ability to analyze the statements made in the passage based on the introduction of new information.

Passage II (Questions 8–13)

Read the following passage, and then answer the questions.

Paragraph 1

The flow of ions must be regulated in order for a neuron to function properly. While at rest, "leaky" ion channels stay open to maintain a constant resting potential. Then, during an action potential, voltage-gated ion channels are responsible for dramatic changes in membrane potential.

This first paragraph can be considered a "background information" paragraph. It contains no information that you shouldn't already know from your science classes, but it serves to introduce the topic of the passage (neuron action potentials) and clue you in to what physics and chemistry topics might be covered later on. (If ions, charge, and electrostatics aren't your personal strong suits, you might choose to skip past this passage on Test Day and come back later if you have extra time at the end of the section.) Now, let's move on to Paragraph 2.

Paragraph 2

The myelin sheath, which also facilitates the proper flow of charge in a neuron, is analogous to the insulating cover over an electrical wire and is composed of oligodendrocytes in the CNS and Schwann cells in the PNS. These cells wrap around the axon several times, creating a multiple layers of insulation. The primary role of the myelin sheath is to conserve charge and increase the conduction velocity of the action potential. The myelin sheath increases the conduction velocity by both increasing the resistance of the membrane and decreasing its capacitance. Interruptions in the myelin sheath are called Nodes of Ranvier (NR). The voltage-gated ion channels are located at these nodes. When an action potential occurs at one node, it quickly travels to depolarize the next node and this pattern continues down the axon.

Now we're learning about the "major characters" of this passage, which are oligodendrocytes, Schwann cells, axons, the myelin sheath, and Nodes of Ranvier. More parallels are also being drawn to physics principles, as can be seen by the words "insulation," "conduction," "charge," "resistance," "capacitance," and "voltage." These are all clues from the testmaker, telling us exactly what concepts will be tested in the questions. This confirms our predictions from the first paragraph: electrostatics and circuits, here we come!

The rest of the passage—Paragraph 3 and beyond—covers most of the new science introduced by the passage and shows us some pretty intense equations.

Paragraph 3, Equation 1, Equation 2

Equation 1, a form of the Nernst equation, can be used to find the electric potential of an ion across the cellular membrane. V_m represents the membrane potential; $[x]_{out}$ and $[x]_{in}$ are the extracellular and intracellular concentrations, respectively, of the ion in question; and z is the integer value of the charge of the ion.

$$V_m = \left(\frac{61.5}{z} \right) \log \left(\frac{[x]_{out}}{[x]_{in}} \right)$$

Equation 1

The Goldman-Hodgkin-Katz equation, Equation 2, combines all of the ions relevant to an action potential into one equation. In a neuron, V_m equals about −70 mV at resting potential, but quickly increases, then decreases during an action potential.

$$V_m = 61.5 \, \log \left(\frac{P_{Na^+}[Na^+]_{out} + P_{K^+}[K^+]_{out} + P_{Cl^-}[Cl^-]_{in}}{P_{Na^+}[Na^+]_{in} + P_{K^+}[K^+]_{in} + P_{Cl^-}[Cl^-]_{out}} \right)$$

Equation 2

P_{K^+}, P_{Na^+} and P_{Cl^-} are the ionic permeabilities of K^+, Na^+ and Cl^- respectively. At resting potential the $P_{K^+} : P_{Na^+} : P_{Cl^-}$ ratio is 1 : 0.04 : 0.45.

The MCAT will often use a passage to present you with potentially intimidating equations or chemical reactions. The first step in dealing with this is *not to panic*. On your scratch paper, where you take notes for these equations, you should write down their purposes and possibly some key variables; go any deeper than that and you'll be wasting valuable time that you could instead spend answering questions.

So in summary, your notes for this passage should look something like this:

Paragraph 1: Ion flow and neuron action potentials; "leaky" channels and voltage-gated channels

Paragraph 2: Voltage-gated channels and myelin details; capacitance, conductance, Nodes of Ranvier

Paragraph 3: Nernst equation calculates membrane potential

Equation 1: Membrane potential equation (general)

Equation 2: Goldman-Hodgkin-Katz equation (specific to action potential)

Now let's look at the questions attached to this passage. Unlike with questions in CARS, we will use the answer choices to help guide our thinking in the three science sections.

Questions

Question 8

When one sodium cation is transferred by Na^+/K^+ ATPase from the intracellular space to the extracellular space, what is its change in electric potential energy, assuming the membrane is at resting potential? (The charge of an electron is approximately -1.602×10^{-19} C.)

    A. -1.12×10^{-20} J
    B. 1.12×10^{-20} J
    C. -8.92×10^{19} J
    D. 8.92×10^{19} J

This question asks for a change in electric potential energy, and so it is answerable by applying the formula for electric potential energy, $U = \Delta Vq$ and executing a calculation using all the numbers given in the question stem. However, this question is also answerable (somewhat more quickly!) by carefully looking at the answer choices and considering the situation. Since we learned in the passage that "resting potential" is about −70 mV, we know the sodium cation is being pumped by the Na⁺/K⁺ ATPase *from* an area whose potential is −70 mV (inside the cell) *to* an area that is at a potential of 0 mV relative to the intracellular space (outside the cell).

So, since both ΔV (the change in voltage) and q (the charge of the sodium cation) are positive, the answer must be a positive value— and this makes sense, because we are moving a *positively charged* particle *away* from a negatively charged environment, which we know will increase potential energy. This all allows us to eliminate choices (A) and (C).

Then, choice (D) can also be eliminated because its value, on the order of 10^{19} joules, is *far* too large to be the answer to a question about microscopic nerve cells. Therefore, by process of elimination, **answer choice (B)** must be correct.

Question 9

In the myelinated portions of a neuron, current can only be dissipated from the intracellular space if it travels through the cell membrane and all the layers of myelin until it finally reaches the extracellular space. How does this information affect the claims made in the passage?

    A.   It weakens the claim that the myelin sheath acts to decrease the capacitance because capacitors in series have a higher net capacitance.

    B.   It strengthens the claim that the myelin sheath acts to decrease the capacitance because capacitors in series have a lower net capacitance.

    C.   It weakens that claim that the myelin sheath acts to decrease the capacitance because capacitors in parallel have a higher net capacitance.

    D.   It strengthens the claim that the myelin sheath acts to decrease the capacitance because capacitors in parallel have a lower net capacitance.

Both the question stem and answer choices are very long and wordy here. But with calm analysis, you can see that the "claim in the passage" referred to in the question stem is this statement: "The myelin sheath increases the conduction velocity ... decreasing its capacitance." And the answer choices depend on the answer to two binary questions: one, whether the layers of myelin on a cell act as capacitors in series or in parallel, and two, whether wiring capacitors in series or parallel increases or decreases net capacitance.

Let's answer the first question first. The passage (in the second paragraph) states, "these cells wrap around the axons several times, creating multiple layers of insulation," and the question stem states that current can only be dissipated if it travels through "all the multiple layers of myelin." Both of these clues imply that the multiple myelin layers will act as capacitors in *series*, not in parallel. That means you can eliminate choices (C) and (D).

Now, to finally answer the question, we have to remember how capacitors act in series, which is something you should know from your college physics course. Wiring capacitors in series actually *lowers* the net capacitance of the circuit, so **answer choice (B)** is correct.

Question 10

When the extracellular concentration of each ion in the Goldman-Hodgkin-Katz equation is proportionally increased, the ion concentration that would cause the greatest change in the resting membrane potential is:

A. the K^+ gradient.
B. the Na^+ gradient.
C. the Cl^- gradient.
D. none of them; each gradient would have an equal effect.

The question actually gives away the best tool for answering it; it directs you to the Goldman-Hodgkin-Katz (GHK) equation, which is Equation 2 in the passage. In the text just after the equation, we're given the relative values for P_{K^+}, P_{Na^+} and P_{Cl^-}, which are the ionic permeabilities of the three ions in the equation, and are also used as coefficients in the GHK equation. The largest of these (at a value of 1 in the ratio that ends the passage) is P; since the question stem says that the extracellular concentrations of the three ions are increased proportionally, the gradient of K^+ will have the largest impact on the final value of V_m, as $[K^+]_{out}$ will have the largest coefficient of the three ion concentrations in the equation. **Answer choice (A)** is correct.

Question 11

If a membrane was constructed whose membrane potential relied on the concentration of only chloride ions, which of the following internal and external ion concentrations, respectively, would result in a membrane potential of 123 mV?

A. 10 mM, 1 mM
B. 5 mM, 500 mM
C. 500 mM, 5 mM
D. 2 mM, 2 M

As stated in the passage, the Nernst equation (Equation 2) can be used to calculate the membrane potential when only one ion is involved. Plugging in the given membrane potential of 123 mV and the charge of the chloride ion, −1, into $V_m = (61.5/z) \times \log([x]_{out}/[x]_{in})$, we get

$$123 \text{ mV} = -61.5 \times \log([x]_{out}/[x]_{in})$$

which can be rearranged using the rules of logarithms (which the testmakers expect you to know) to

$$123 \text{ mV} = 61.5 \times \log([x]_{in}/[x]_{out}).$$

By dividing both sides by 61.5, this can be simplified to

$$2 = \log([x]_{in}/[x]_{out}).$$

Finally, our knowledge of logarithms tells us that $\log(100) = 2$. Therefore, the ratio of $[Cl^-]_{in}:[Cl^-]_{out}$ must be 100:1. **Answer choice (B)**, a concentration of 500 mM inside and 5 mM outside, matches this ratio and is therefore correct.

TEST DAY TIP

The level of math required in Question 11, including the knowledge that $\log(100) = 2$, is within the bounds of what the AAMC will expect of your mathematical knowledge.

Question 12

Hypokalemia (low blood concentration of potassium) affects the resting membrane potential of a neuron. Which of the following is most likely to be observed in the neurons of a patient with hypokalemia?

A. There will be depolarization of the resting membrane potential, requiring more stimulus to cause an action potential.

B. There will be hyperpolarization of the resting membrane potential, requiring more stimulus to cause an action potential.

C. There will be hyperpolarization of the resting membrane potential, requiring less stimulus to cause an action potential.

D. There will be depolarization of the resting membrane potential, requiring less stimulus to cause an action potential.

We learn from the question stem that hypokalemia is a low *blood* concentration of potassium, which means the *extracellular* K^+ concentration is lowered. When the extracellular K^+ concentration is lowered, the resting membrane potential of a neuron is made more negative—this is called hyperpolarization, and more polarization means that more stimulus is required to cause an action potential. (Depolarization, on the other hand, is act of making the potential less negative and more positive.) This means that **answer choice (B)** is correct.

But let's see why this is, using the equations in the passage to back ourselves up. The effect of ion concentrations on the membrane potential can be seen mathematically with the GHK equation, which is Equation 2 in the passage. We know from the last paragraph of the passage that the resting potential is negative, so at resting potential the right side of the GHK equation must be the logarithm of a value between 0 and 1. This means the sum of the values in the numerator must be less than the sum of the values in the denominator. From this starting point, lowering the $[K^+]_{out}$ would make the fraction even smaller (closer to 0), making the logarithm of that number more negative.

Question 13

If the width of the plasma membrane is approximately 5 nm, what is the electrostatic force acting on a sodium cation as it passes from the extracellular space to the intracellular space through a "leaky" sodium channel at resting potential? (The charge of an electron is approximately -1.602×10^{-19} C.)

A. 1.3×10^{-12} N
B. 2.2×10^{-12} N
C. 1.3×10^{-10} N
D. 2.2×10^{-10} N

Answering this question requires applying two equations. First, we'll calculate the electric field across the cell membrane using the equation $\Delta V = Ed$. From the passage, we are told that the typical neuronal membrane resting potential is −70 mV, and so moving from inside to the cell to outside it (as the sodium ion is in this question stem), we travel over a potential difference of +70 mV. (Remember that it is standard procedure to set the extracellular environment as the reference point of 0 mV). We are also told in the question stem that the cell membrane is 5 nm thick, which means we can now calculate E. Plugging in our values we get:

$$\Delta V = Ed$$

$$(7 \times 10^{-2} \text{ V}) = E \times (5 \times 10^{-9} \text{ m})$$

$$(7 \times 10^{-2} \text{ V}) / (5 \times 10^{-9} \text{ m}) = E$$

$$E = 1.4 \times 10^{7} \text{ N/C}$$

We can now use the equation $F = Eq$ to calculate electrostatic force (F) using the E we just found and the charge of an electron (given in the question stem). The charge on an electron can be used (but as a positive number) because the sodium cation has a positive charge equal to one electron; this is because the cation lost exactly one electron to become an ion. This gives us:

$$F = Eq$$

$$F = (1.4 \times 10^7 \text{ N/C}) (1.602 \times 10^{-19} \text{ C})$$

$$F = 2.2 \times 10^{-12} \text{ N}$$

This matches with **answer choice (B)**. Note that you don't have to find the exact solution yourself to solve here—simply approximating the solutions to tough calculations will be enough to confidently choose choice (B), as there is no other answer choice that is very close to it.

Discrete Questions

Every science section of MCAT 2015 will include some discrete questions (some call them "stand-alone" questions) that are not attached to a passage. Let's look at two of them: one organic chemistry question and one experiment-based biochemistry question.

MCAT FACTS

Although the AAMC has not given exact specifications on how many questions on MCAT 2015 that will be discrete, it is safe to assume that about one-quarter of science questions will be discretes; that's the ratio for the current MCAT.

Question 14

The mutant gene that causes Huntington's disease contains an increased variable number of CAG trinucleotide repeats. The codon CAG codes for glutamine, whose structure is shown below.

Overabundance of glutamine results in protein aggregation, which leads to neuronal degradation. Which type of intermolecular force is primarily responsible for this protein aggregation?

A.   Debye forces
B.   Dispersion forces
C.   Dipole-dipole interactions
D.   Hydrogen bonding

To solve this question, we need to know the definition of each of the intermolecular forces, as well as their relative strengths. From examining the structure of glutamine, we see that the side chain has an amide functional group. This side chain is polar and in particular, is capable of hydrogen bonding, since it contains a hydrogen bonded to a nitrogen. Hydrogen bonding, **answer choice (D)**, is the most powerful intermolecular force present, and thus is the primary reason that these proteins aggregate. Note that intermolecular forces other than hydrogen bonding (especially dipole-dipole interactions) will also be present, but hydrogen bonding will still be "primarily responsible" for the aggregation because it is the strongest, and that's what the question stem asks us for.

Question 15

In a 1973 experiment, Christian Anfinsen converted ribonuclease A to an inactive enzyme by reducing the disulfide bonds with a reducing reagent and then denaturing the compound with 8 M urea. Then, upon slow removal of the urea, the protein regained its native structure and over 90% activity, leading Anfinsen to conclude that the three-dimensional fold of a protein is solely determined by its primary structure. One objection to this conclusion was that the RNAse A may not have been completely unfolded in 8 M urea. What modification to the experiment could be made to address this objection?

A. Add another unfolding reagent to the urea mixture, remove all reagents, and examine the resulting activity.

B. Use a more effective reducing agent, remove all reagents, and examine the resulting activity.

C. Increase the urea concentration to 16 M, remove all reagents, and examine the resulting activity.

D. Oxidize the RNAse A before urea removal to restore disulfide bonds and examine the resulting activity.

While the large restoration of enzyme activity (>90%) observed by Anfinsen is suggestive of the enzyme going from completely unfolded and inactive to fully folded and active, it is genuinely possible, as the critics in the question stem assert, that the enzyme still retained some activity in 8 M urea. The only way to figure out whether the enzyme is somewhat urea-stable is to determine its activity before removing the urea. To do this, we would have to make sure that the disulfide bonds get reformed, however, before doing an activity test. Therefore, oxidizing the RNAse in order to reform the disulfide bonds—remember that oxidation will create disulfide bonds from 2 –SH groups to form some of a protein's tertiary or quaternary structure—is a key step that must be completed before doing any in-urea activity measurement. This is what **answer choice (D)** says, so it is correct.

TEST DAY TIP

If this question seems difficult, then you've got a good eye! This is just about the most reading and reasoning the MCAT 2015 will demand from you in a single question. It's also a good example of how MCAT 2015 will test experimental and research design on the Chem/Phys and Bio/Biochem sections.

The Chem/Phys section of the MCAT 2015, while similar to the current MCAT's Physical Sciences section in many ways, will also be different in other important ways, each of which has been illustrated by this question set. Namely, the new section will test chemistry and physics only within the context of biological systems, and the section will also include organic chemistry and biochemistry.

This means that success on the section means much more than just recalling your physics and chemistry courses from college. It means that between now and Test Day you have to learn specific best strategies for MCAT 2015, and get lots of test-like practice with the particular contexts and subject combinations you'll find on the official exam.

BIOLOGICAL AND BIOCHEMICAL FOUNDATIONS OF LIVING SYSTEMS (BIO/BIOCHEM)

As aspiring physicians, you will probably be most familiar with the subject matter in the Biological and Biochemical Foundations of Living Systems, or Bio/Biochem, section of MCAT 2015. Although the AAMC has promised to make a deliberate effort to make all sections of the new MCAT more relevant to what students will see in medical school, this will be especially pronounced in the Bio/Biochem section. However, it is important that you don't confuse your potential interest in the topics of the section with knowledge on how to answer the questions successfully. That success can only come from the right kind of targeted practice with test-like materials.

Fortunately, that practice will be eminently available to you by the time you take your test, and we'll start the process right here. Since the biggest change to the Bio/Biochem section of MCAT 2015 is the additional testing of biochemistry content, we will start our focused review of test-like Bio/Biochem content by dissecting a typical biochemistry passage and its associated questions.

TEST DAY TIP

While biochemistry is an important part of the Bio/Biochem section, it is not the only place that you will encounter this content on Test Day. In the *Preview Guide for the MCAT²⁰¹⁵ Exam*, the AAMC explicitly states that there will be biochemistry content in the Chem/Phys section as well.

Passage III (Questions 16–21)

Read the following passage, and then answer the questions.

Paragraph 1

Vitamin B_{12} (cobalamin) deficiency is one of the most common causes of anemia worldwide. The symptoms of vitamin B_{12} deficiency usually present similar to other forms of anemia such as iron deficiency anemia and folate deficiency anemia, in that patients are often fatigued and may experience weakness, general malaise, and sometimes shortness of breath on exertion. However, with long-standing vitamin B_{12} deficiency, patients may present with additional symptoms—psychological and neurological problems, often as permanent conditions. This occurs when excessive methylmalonic acid incorporates into fatty membranes, causing fragility of the membrane and leakage of electrolytes.

Now, that wasn't so bad, was it? The paragraph begins by introducing what will likely be the overall topic for the entire passage, vitamin B_{12} deficiency. The first few sentences give real-world background information that is only indirectly related to the science in the passage. This information is generally not assessed by questions on the science sections of the MCAT, so we should read through those sentences quickly, without worrying about the details. However, we do need to pay attention to the last few lines where the author explains the cause of permanent psychological and neurological problems—too much methylmalonic acid, which results in fragile membranes and electrolyte leakage. In fact, the last sentence represents a very testable concept. Given this information, we should anticipate that Paragraph 2 might be more discussion of vitamin B_{12} deficiency. Let's tackle it next.

Paragraph 2

Vitamin B_{12} deficiency is more widespread in the developing world since it is rare for people in the developed world to lack vitamin B_{12} in their diets. Most often those who do are elderly. This is because atrophic gastritis, a common ailment in the elderly, impairs the stomach's secretion of intrinsic factor. Intrinsic factor, a glycoprotein produced by the stomach, binds to vitamin B_{12} in the alkaline environment of the duodenum. Vitamin B_{12} must be attached to intrinsic factor for it to be absorbed correctly.

In this paragraph, the author presents two key phrases: "atrophic gastritis" and "intrinsic factor." Atrophic gastritis is important only in that it bridges the discussion on vitamin B_{12} deficiency in the elderly with the true star of the paragraph, intrinsic factor. The details given about intrinsic factor in this paragraph, along with the word "must" in the last sentence, should be seen as clues that we will likely see this concept again in the questions.

Paragraph 3, Figure 1

Cobalamin is crucial for the metabolism in every cell of the body, and especially for DNA synthesis and regulation. It is especially important for tissues with high turnover such as bone marrow-derived cells and gastrointestinal mucosa. A blood smear of the red blood

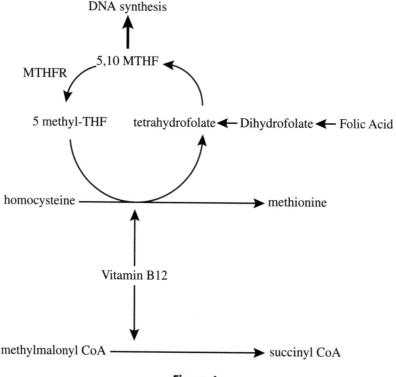

Figure 1

cells in a vitamin B_{12}-deficient individual would show megaloblastic anemia (abnormally large red blood cells) because of excessive mRNA production. Figure 1 shows how activated vitamin B_{12} helps synthesize tetrahydrofolate, which is essential for methylating DNA during DNA synthesis.

Our first job in this paragraph is to remember (from Paragraph 1) that cobalamin is another name for vitamin B_{12}. After that, it's important to realize that every sentence of this paragraph contains testable information, including vitamin B_{12}'s role in DNA synthesis, high turnover tissues, and megaloblastic anemia. Things really get interesting when we are directed to Figure 1 which essentially shows the mechanism that makes vitamin B_{12} invaluable during DNA synthesis.

Paragraph 4, Table 1

Four patients with suspected vitamin B_{12} deficiency were given oral vitamin B_{12} supplements, recombinant intrinsic factor, and vitamin B_{12} intramuscular injections in 4-week trials. Serum levels of vitamin B_{12} posttreatment are tabulated in Table 1.

Patient	Oral Vitamin B_{12} Supplement	Recombinant Intrinsic Factor	Vitamin B_{12} Intramuscular Injection
1	↑	↑	↑
2	↔	↑	↑
3	↔	↔	↑
4	↔	↔	↔

Table 1: Serum levels of vitamin B_{12} posttreatment.

Aha! After all of that information, we finally see that this is actually an experimental passage. Given MCAT 2015's new emphasis on research and analysis, we can bet that many of this passage's questions will come from this paragraph and its associated table. In order to gain the most points from the questions, we must understand the primary purpose of the experiment: to analyze the effects of 3 different forms of vitamin B_{12} replacement therapy. In this passage, we also have the benefit of having a table that displays the results of the experiment for quick analysis.

On Test Day, it will be good practice to take some brief notes on each paragraph. Here is an example of what that summary could look like:

Paragraph 1: Effects of vitamin B_{12} deficiency, excess methylmalonic acid $\rightarrow$ fragile membrane

Paragraph 2: Role of intrinsic factor in vitamin B_{12} absorption

Paragraph 3: Vitamin B_{12}'s function in cells' metabolism and DNA synthesis

Figure 1: Mechanism of vitamin B_{12}'s role in DNA synthesis

Paragraph 4: Experiment testing vitamin B_{12} replacement therapies

Table 1: Results of experiment

Armed with this strategic dissection of the passage, we are now ready to tackle the questions associated with it.

TEST DAY TIP

Given that MCAT 2015 has such long, dense passages, the practice of jotting down very brief notes as you work through the paragraphs can be a very practical one. Taking notes will help you integrate the material as you read, and it will also give you a useful reference tool for answering the questions.

Questions

Question 16

Folate deficiency anemia can be confused with vitamin B_{12} deficiency anemia since both result in abnormally large red blood cells. In order to differentiate between the two, physicians may check the serum levels of methylmalonic acid (a precursor to methylmalonyl CoA) and homocysteine. How does this help distinguish the two types of anemia?

A. If the patient were folic acid deficient, he or she would have elevated serum levels of both homocysteine and methylmalonic acid.

B. If the patient were folic acid deficient, he or she would have elevated serum levels of homocysteine and normal levels of methylmalonic acid.

C. If the patient were vitamin B_{12} deficient, he or she would have normal levels of homocysteine and elevated levels of methylmalonic acid.

D. If the patient were vitamin B_{12} deficient, he or she would have normal levels of homocysteine and elevated levels of methylmalonic acid.

From the answer choices, we can see that we have to analyze the relationship between methylmalonic acid and its derivatives for the correct answer. Looking at our notes from the passage, we know that Figure 1 has the information that we need. Figure 1 shows that vitamin B_{12} is needed to convert homocysteine to methionine and methylmalonyl CoA to succinyl CoA. Thus, in a patient with vitamin B_{12} deficiency, we would expect the serum levels of *both* homocysteine and methylmalonic acid to be elevated. So, let's look through the answer choices to see which one works best. Unfortunately, there's no perfect match to this in the answer choices, but we can determine that the correct answer is **answer choice (B)** by using our prediction to eliminate the other choices. Since Figure 1 demonstrates that in a vitamin B_{12} deficiency we would expect the serum levels of *both* homocysteine and methylmalonic acid to be elevated, we can eliminate choices (C) and (D). Furthermore, the question states that physicians check serum levels of methylmalonic acid and homocysteine in order to differentiate between the two vitamin deficiencies. This implies that if vitamin B_{12} deficiency leads to elevated levels of both homocysteine and methylmalonic acid, folate deficiency will not have similar serum level results. Therefore, choice (A) can be eliminated as well, and we can be sure that choice (B) is correct.

Question 17

It can be inferred from the passage that vitamin B_{12} is essential for which part of the nervous system?

A. neurotransmitter packaging
B. RNA synthesis regulation
C. Na^+/K^+ pump
D. myelin sheath

Paragraph 1 states that the nervous system is affected when methylmalonic acid is incorporated into fatty membranes in excessive amounts. The correct answer would have to be something that is highly dependent on fatty membranes. Given the answer choices, the myelin sheath, which is composed predominantly of lipids, is the part of the nervous system most likely affected by a change in the fatty membranes, and hence **answer choice (D)** is correct. Choice (A) can be eliminated because, although methionine is a precursor to many neurotransmitters, vitamin B_{12} is not essential for *packaging* the neurotransmitters. Choice (B) can be eliminated because, while paragraph 3 does mention that there would be excessive RNA synthesis in vitamin B_{12} deficiency, RNA synthesis regulation is a general metabolic process and is not specific to the nervous system. Finally, choice (C) can be eliminated because, even though it says that leakage of electrolytes occurs when methylmalonic acid is incorporated into the fatty membrane, we cannot assume this to mean that the leakage occurs via the Na^+/K^+ pump.

Question 18

According to the passage, which of the following patients would most likely require a lifetime of vitamin B_{12} injections as a treatment for vitamin B_{12} deficiency?

    A.   A patient with high titers of antiparietal cell antibodies
    B.   A patient who has severe pancreatic insufficiency
    C.   A patient who has had his or her gallbladder removed
    D.   A patient who has had his or her entire colon removed

Glancing at the answer choices, we see different types of ailments. To tackle this question, we must test the feasibility of each choice given the information in the passage.

First, let's look at choice (A) and the possibility of treating someone with high titers of antiparietal cell antibodies with a lifetime of vitamin B_{12} injections. From the passage and our general content knowledge, we can infer that intrinsic factor, an alkaline environment in the duodenum, and adequate surface area are all needed to absorb vitamin B_{12} efficiently. If there were high titers of antiparietal cell antibodies, then the production of intrinsic factor would be cut off. Since we can infer from Table 1 that these patients can be treated with supplemental intrinsic factor, choice (A) should not require a lifetime of vitamin B_{12} injections, because the problem lies in the production of intrinsic factor, not in vitamin B_{12} absorption.

Choice (B) features a patient with severe pancreatic insufficiency. Such a patient would not be able to produce bicarbonate, the primary solute used to increase the pH of the duodenum after gastric emptying. This would hinder absorption of vitamin B_{12}, since vitamin B_{12} can bind with intrinsic factor only in alkaline conditions. Hence the patient in choice (B) will benefit from a lifetime of vitamin B_{12} injections, because that will allow the patient to have vitamin B_{12} in his or her bloodstream without being absorbed in the usual way. **Answer choice (B)** is correct.

Let's quickly look at why choices (C) and (D) are incorrect. The only purpose of the gallbladder is to store bile, and bile is not essential for absorbing vitamin B_{12}. Therefore, a patient with his or her gallbladder removed would have no trouble absorbing vitamin B_{12}, and choice (C) is incorrect. Choice (D) is incorrect because the colon is not a primary source of vitamin absorption (some water- and fat-soluble vitamins are absorbed in the colon, but vitamin B_{12} is not one of those vitamins).

Question 19

Which step of protein synthesis is most likely to be affected in a patient with megaloblastic anemia?

 A. Transcription
 B. Translation
 C. Methylation
 D. Splicing

Using the brief notes that we took while reading the passage, we know that megaloblastic anemia is discussed in Paragraph 3. We can quickly review the paragraph and learn that excessive amounts of mRNA are produced in a person suffering from megaloblastic anemia. Thus, we are looking for an answer that is directly related to production of mRNA. Therefore, **answer choice (A)** is correct because transcription is the production of mRNA from DNA.

The other choices are all incorrect because they are not as directly involved in mRNA synthesis. Translation, choice (B), is the building of the protein from the template of the mRNA which is *after* mRNA production. Methylation, choice (C), may seem enticing since tetrahydrofolate is affected in vitamin B_{12} and folate deficiencies; however, methylation of DNA is affected, not the protein, RNA, or synthesis of protein. And splicing, choice (D), is a posttranscriptional process which is *after* mRNA production.

Question 20

In Table 1, which of the following can most likely be concluded about Patient 2?

    A. The patient is not getting enough vitamin B_{12} in his or her diet.
    B. The patient's body produces antibodies against intrinsic factor.
    C. The patient's body produces antibodies against parietal cells.
    D. The patient's stomach has a pathologically high pH level.

According to Table 1, Patient 2's serum levels of vitamin B_{12} increased upon receiving supplemental recombinant intrinsic factor. This suggests that the patient is not making enough intrinsic factor. This can be confirmed by the fact that Patient 2's serum levels of vitamin B_{12} increased when given intramuscular injections of vitamin B_{12}, but not with oral administration of vitamin B_{12}. Generally, intramuscular injections of vitamin B_{12} are a quick way to get the water-soluble vitamin B_{12} into the bloodstream, bypassing any digestive barriers, and thus the need for intrinsic factor. Orally administered vitamin B_{12}, on the other hand, cannot be absorbed by the body in the absence of intrinsic factor (as stated in Paragraph 2). Thus, based on the results in Table 1, we should predict that the pathology lies in the inability to produce intrinsic factor.

Since parietal cells are the cells in the glands of the stomach that produce intrinsic factor, they are the key to the correct answer. That is, if they are malfunctioning or getting destroyed, the body will be unable to produce intrinsic factor. Thus, **answer choice (C)** is the correct answer. If the patient was not getting enough vitamin B_{12} through the diet, his or her serum levels of vitamin B_{12} would increase after receiving oral supplements. Since this is not the case, choice (A) is incorrect. If the patient's body were producing antibodies against intrinsic factor, he or she would only respond to B_{12} intramuscular injections, and not the recombinant intrinsic factor supplement, since the body would make antibodies against the intrinsic factor supplement too. So, choice (B) is incorrect as well. Finally, from Paragraph 2, we know that intrinsic factor is able to bind to vitamin B_{12} in an alkaline environment. A patient with pathologically high pH level in the stomach will have no problem allowing intrinsic factor to bind to vitamin B_{12} in the stomach, in addition to the binding that takes place normally only in the duodenum. This would actually *aid* absorption of vitamin B_{12} taken orally. However, since Patient 2's serum levels of vitamin B_{12} didn't increase with oral supplements of vitamin B_{12}, choice (D) can be eliminated.

Question 21

Vitamin B_{12} deficiency would most likely cause a significant decrease in the number of:

    A.   B lymphocytes.
    B.   neurons.
    C.   skeletal muscle cells.
    D.   renal cells.

The question is asking us to understand the role of vitamin B_{12} in the body. As we can recall from Paragraph 3, deficiency of vitamin B_{12} especially affects cells that have rapid turnover, such as bone marrow–derived cells and gastrointestinal mucosa. So to arrive at the correct answer, we need to look for cells that fall in either of those categories. B lymphocytes are a perfect example of this; they are white blood cells made in the bone marrow and must be continuously made. Therefore the correct answer is **answer choice (A)**.

As for the incorrect answer choices, we can easily eliminate choice (C), skeletal muscle cells, since their replication is very slow; neurons have the lowest turnover of any cells in the body, and therefore choice (B) is incorrect; and renal cells in the kidney do not undergo as high a turnover as the bone marrow–derived cells and gastrointestinal mucosa, so choice (D) is also incorrect.

Discrete Questions

Congratulations! You have just completed your first passage in the MCAT 2015's new Biological and Biochemical Foundation of Living Systems section. Hopefully you now have a better understanding of how the biochemistry content will be integrated and tested on the new MCAT, and you can begin to appreciate the test-taking skills necessary to attack the passage and questions.

Passage-based questions are not the only type that will appear on MCAT 2015, however. Just like the current MCAT, the 2015 exam will have plenty of discrete questions in the science sections. Here are a couple discretes that could appear in the Bio/Biochem section.

Question 22

Assuming that a "5" on each axis represents normal levels of the hormone, which of the following points would most likely correspond to the hormone levels of an individual with an ACTH-secreting tumor of the anterior pituitary?

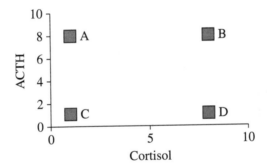

A. A
B. B
C. C
D. D

Looking at the axes on the graph, we can see that the two variables that we are interested in are levels of ACTH and cortisol on the y- and x-axes, respectively. While a tumor of the anterior pituitary could potentially secrete any number of hormones, this question specifies an ACTH-releasing tumor. In order to choose the correct answer, we need to consider the effects of this type of tumor. An ACTH-secreting tumor of the anterior pituitary would cause ACTH to be elevated. Only choice (A) or (B) fulfills this fact. The other factor to consider is cortisol, a major hormone produced by the adrenal cortex. Since the adrenal cortex is the target gland for ACTH, it will respond to the excess amount of ACTH by producing cortisol. Normal negative feedback mechanisms for these hormones will also not work properly because of the unregulated tumor. Therefore, since both hormones will be found in higher concentrations, **answer choice (B)** is correct.

Question 23

As part of a research study determining the levels of antibodies present in a healthy individual's blood, scientists tested randomly selected healthy subjects. They found that out of all the blood samples that did not have the Rh antigen on their red blood cells, 90% did not have significant levels of anti-Rh antibodies in their plasma, but 10% did. What is the most likely reason for the elevated levels of anti-Rh antibodies in the second group?

A. Rh⁻ individuals with autoimmune disease can develop anti-Rh antibodies.

B. If an Rh⁻ individual received an Rh⁺ blood transfusion; his or her immune system would produce anti-Rh antibodies.

C. Rh⁻ women can be exposed to an Rh⁺ infant's blood during pregnancy or childbirth, and can thus develop anti-Rh antibodies.

D. It is normal for Rh⁻ individuals to have anti-Rh antibodies in their blood.

The question is essentially asking to identify a phenomenon that would explain the presence of anti-Rh antibodies in a healthy individual without the presence of Rh antigens on his or her RBCs. Let's read through the answer choices to see which the most plausible is given our knowledge of biological mechanisms.

Choice (A) may be tempting because it seems to have the right language, but it is incorrect because it distorts the topic that is being tested. While it is true that a person suffering from autoimmune hemolytic anemia will produce antibodies against his or her own antigens, this means that an Rh-*positive* person with autoimmune disease would have anti-Rh antibodies in his or her blood. The group being discussed in the question is Rh-*negative*, and hence the group would not have anti-Rh antibodies even if suffering from autoimmune disease. Therefore, choice (A) is incorrect.

Meanwhile, choice (B) incorrectly uses a detail provided in the question stem. If an Rh⁻ person received an Rh⁺ blood transfusion, his or her immune system would immediately produce anti-Rh antibodies and cause agglutination, which can cause severe, even fatal, hemolysis. Since the researchers only selected *healthy* blood samples, this blood sample would be screened out. Also, the chances of such a blood transfusion happening are very remote, so this is not a likely explanation for the question.

That brings us to choice (C). During any pregnancy, a small amount of the baby's blood can enter the mother's circulation. If the mother is Rh⁻ and the baby is Rh⁺, the mother may produce anti-Rh antibodies to combat the Rh antigen in her baby's red blood cells. This is known as erythroblastosis fetalis. Note that the affected female is considered healthy and will show no symptoms unless she has any subsequent Rh⁺ pregnancies. Therefore, **answer choice (C)** is the correct answer.

For completeness, let's look at choice (D). This is simply untrue—a person with Rh⁻ blood does not have anti-Rh antibodies naturally in the blood plasma. But a person with Rh⁻ blood can *develop* anti-Rh antibodies in the blood plasma if he or she receives blood from a person with Rh⁺ blood, whose Rh antigens can trigger the production of anti-Rh antibodies. This is unlike the A and B antibodies, incidentally; a person without A and B antigens (i.e., blood group O) will normally have both A and B antibodies in the blood.

And with that we have come to the end of our practice material on the Bio/Biochem section of the MCAT 2015. With so many changes coming to the test, it is helpful to know that biology and the various mechanisms that make life possible are always constant. Therefore, most of the content you learn in your biology courses will always have some relevance to standardized exams like the MCAT. Just remember that, as with every other section on MCAT 2015, targeted practice and strategy will be vital to your success on Test Day. Fortunately, with this review you are now one step closer!

PSYCHOLOGICAL, SOCIAL, AND BIOLOGICAL FOUNDATIONS OF BEHAVIOR (PSYCH/SOC)

This section will contain the most new content out of any section of MCAT 2015. This content addition is in response to the changing face of medical care. The goal of this section is to evaluate test takers on their ability to use critical reasoning skills in the context of sociology and psychology. As sociocultural and behavioral aspects are analyzed more frequently in healthcare, so must incoming medical students be prepared for this portion of their curriculum and eventual career. So yes, there will be full classes that many of you will have to take in order to prepare for this section. However, when you end up acing this section on your MCAT, you will be a very competitive applicant because of the importance given to these topics.

Let's take a look at a passage, paragraph by paragraph, to see how to best think through passages on the new Psychological, Social, and Biological Foundations of Behavior section.

Passage IV (Questions 24–29)

Read the following passage, and then answer the questions.

Paragraph 1, Table 1

> A graduate student read about the unreliability of eyewitness accounts and decided to perform a study exploring false memories. She designed an experiment that tested whether actively trying to remember an experience affects one's ability to accurately remember that experience. She decided to test the experience of listening to a series of four groups of related words. These words are listed in decreasing power of association in Table 1.

We can see from the first sentence that this passage will be about a psychological experiment, so we know to keep track of the methods, and the reasoning behind those methods. In this first paragraph we get just a little background information and then a description of the material of the study: word lists. This means the experimental procedure should follow in Paragraph 2.

Chair	River	Soft	Thief
Table	Water	Hard	Steal
Sit	Stream	Light	Robber
Legs	Lake	Pillow	Crook
Seat	Mississippi	Plush	Burglar
Couch	Boat	Loud	Money
Desk	Tide	Cotton	Cop
Recliner	Swim	Fur	Bad
Sofa	Flow	Touch	Rob
Wood	Run	Fluffy	Jail
Cushion	Barge	Feather	Gun
Swivel	Creek	Furry	Villain
Stool	Brook	Downy	Crime
Sitting	Fish	Kitten	Bank
Rocking	Bridge	Skin	Bandit
Bench	Winding	Tender	Criminal

Table 1: Seed Words and associated words lists, organized by power of association.

Paragraph 2

During the experiment, each test subject listened to a list of ten words that were randomly selected from the first 12 entries of a given word list. The Seed Words were not read. The subjects were then randomly directed either to spend 3 minutes thinking about the list of words they just heard, or to spend 3 minutes solving basic arithmetic problems. This process of listening followed by either a recall session or a math session was repeated for each of the four lists. The presentation order of the four lists was randomized.

And here is the experimental procedure we predicted we would find. The great thing about experimental procedures outlined on the MCAT is that you don't have to understand them right away. Your goal in this paragraph, and any paragraph where you are simply given the steps of an experiment, is just to write a quick note to remind yourself that this particular experiment is where the methods are. See the following for examples of these notes. Now, move on to the next paragraph.

Paragraph 3, Table 2

After the subjects completed the 4 cycles and heard 40 words, they were handed a sheet of paper with 80 words printed on the page in a random order. Included were the 40 words the subjects heard, along with words from several other categories. There were 12 "Critical Lure" words, which included the Seed Words and the 2 words from the first 12 entries of the list not read aloud. There were 12 "Non-critical Lure" words, which were the last 3, and therefore the most weakly related words from each list. There were also 16 "Unrelated Lure" words, which were chosen because they had no relation to any of the 4 Seed Words. Subjects were asked identify the words previously heard by circling the words on a page. Overall results are shown in Table 2.

	Overall Proportion Reported as "Heard"		
Word Type	**Recall Session**	**Math Session**	**_p_-Value**
Heard	.72	.60	<0.001
Critical Lure	.81	.72	<0.001
Non-Crit. Lure	.52	.44	<0.001
Unrelated Lure	.01	.03	<0.05

Table 2: Proportion of words reported as heard.

Again, this is another paragraph with a lot of steps. So the goal would be to jot a note that this paragraph outlines how the results were generated, and then to go on to the questions. Of course, you will most likely have to come back to the passage and pull certain details from these procedural paragraphs. However, you don't need to do that until you find out which particular details the questions cover. If you spend a lot of time reading and understanding the whole experiment, you're likely going to have wasted your time on Test Day figuring out details for which you won't get any points. So let's move on to the questions, and get those points.

Like in the other sections, it's helpful to create a short list of notes while you read so you can navigate the passage more easily if you have to come back to the text to answer a question:

Paragraph 1: Goal and word lists

Table 1: Word lists

Paragraph 2: Method specifics, categories, and types of words

Paragraph 3: Data calculation

Table 2: Recall proportions of different word types/categories

Questions

Question 24

In this experiment, which area of the brain is responsible for the subject's ability to perceive the presented words?

    A.   Occipital lobe
    B.   Temporal lobe
    C.   Parietal lobe
    D.   Broca's area

Like with all primary sensory areas, perception happens in the cortex and not at any intermediate location. The words were presented in auditory format; it is the temporal lobe that is primarily responsible for perceiving and interpreting sound information. This matches with **answer choice (B)**. Choice (A), the occipital lobe, handles vision. Choice (C), the parietal lobe, helps process spatial orientation and integrating sensory information into a cohesive experience. Finally, choice (D), Broca's area, handles speech production, not perception.

Let's take a look at the next question, which delves into the statistical side of the research.

Question 25

For the recall session group, the graduate student compared the "Heard" and "Critical Lure" proportions. She found $p = 0.02$, suggesting which of the following?

A. The chance she committed a Type I error is 2%.
B. There is a 2% chance that her null hypothesis is true.
C. If she repeated her experiment, she would achieve the same results 98% of the time.
D. If she wanted a 95% confidence level, she could reject this null hypothesis.

A p-value can do one of two things. It either lets you reject the null hypothesis, or fail to reject the null hypothesis. Failing to reject the null is not the same as the null being true. In this case, the null hypothesis (also referred to as H_0) is that the "Heard" and "Critical Lure" frequencies are actually the same, and any differences that showed up in the results are within the normal variation. Finding a p-value of 0.02 means that the graduate student can, with a 95% confidence level, reject the null hypothesis and claim that the "Heard" and "Critical Lure" frequencies are, indeed, different. She could reject H_0 with any $p < 0.05$ at the 95% confidence level.

If, instead, she found a $p = 0.12$ she could not reject the null at 95% confidence ($p > 0.05$). However, failing to reject H_0 does not mean that H_0 is true, like in choice (B). The "Heard" and "Critical Lure" categories may still be different in actuality, but the student cannot claim they are different with 95% confidence. She could make the claim with 85% confidence ($p < 0.15$), but typically one expects confidence levels of 95% or 99% (or even higher).

The p-value does not equal the chance of a Type I error (the H_0 was true, but rejected), as mentioned in choice (A) or a Type II error (H_0 was not rejected even though it was incorrect). The p-value has nothing to do with the likelihood of getting the same results if you repeat the study, as mentioned in choice (C). Thus, **answer choice (D) is correct.**

And with that point achieved, let's look at the next question, which discusses memory.

Question 26

In the study outlined in the passage, which type of memory was tested?

    A.   Working memory
    B.   Sensory memory
    C.   Long-term memory
    D.   Procedural memory

The concept of "short-term memory" was refined by the Baddeley-Hitch model of "working memory" in 1974. It is "working memory" that this study is testing—**answer choice (A)**. Sensory memory, choice (B), holds a brief trace of all sensory input of a given system (different sensory memory for vision, sound, etc.) until the subconscious decides which inputs to "save" in working memory and which to discard. Sensory memory would include the sound of the HVAC system, the hum of the florescent lights, etc. These words weren't tested for recall at a later date, so the answer isn't choice (C), long-term memory. Choice (D), procedural memory is out, because this research isn't testing the memory of performance of an action.

On to the next question, which draws on critical reasoning skills.

Question 27

What criticism could be made of this study?

    A.   This study only shows correlation between recall sessions and generation of false memories, and therefore cannot demonstrate causation.
    B.   This study used auditory input to form a memory and then visual input to stimulate recall; mixing these two sensory inputs may have had a confounding effect on the results.
    C.   Ethical concerns regarding subjecting people to stressful situations and then testing the accuracy of their memory are outweighed by the benefits of increased knowledge of short-term memory accuracy in eyewitness accounts.
    D.   Basic arithmetic and language skills are handled by separate hemispheres, so the effect on memory formation and recall after complete basic math problems is negligible.

Mixing different processing centers in the brain may have an effect on memory formation not explored by this study (even though this study introduces this discrepancy without controlling for it). The study would have been better if it either used both visual stimulation to trigger a memory and trigger recall, or both auditory stimulation to trigger a memory and trigger recall. If a sizable number of patients were blind or deaf, this would affect the results. **Answer choice (B)** is correct. The other statements are incorrect. For choice (A), randomness helps to support the idea that causation could play a role here. In choice (C), ethical concerns always win when designing a research study. Finally, for choice (D), language and arithmetic skills are usually left-brain dominant functions.

Now we will move to Question 28, which talks about a specific molecule's effect.

Question 28

This study used healthy participants. If a study used participants with thiamine deficiency instead, which of the following cognitive dysfunctions would one most expect to observe?

    A.   Alzheimer's disease
    B.   Down syndrome
    C.   Korsakoff's syndrome
    D.   Parkinson's disease

Korsakoff's syndrome, **answer choice (C)**, has 6 major signs/symptoms (including anterograde and retrograde amnesia, apathy, and confabulation)—all of the 6 symptoms are brought on by thiamine deficiency, typically found in chronic alcoholics and those who are severely malnourished. The other disorders listed are not associated with vitamin B_1 (thiamine) deficiency. Choice (A), Alzheimer's disease, is a disorder of the brain with an essentially unknown cause marked by a progressive decrease in short-term memory and memory consolidation. Choice (B), Down syndrome, has to do with chromosome nondisjunction and includes mild to moderate mental retardation in addition to a number of physical findings. Finally, choice (D), Parkinson's disease, is a disorder of the central nervous system and is usually idiopathic (having no known cause), and usually includes slow movement, a shuffling gait, and difficulty initiating and stopping actions.

Finally, we get to the last question of the passage, which discusses a new topic, prejudice.

Question 29

In addition to memory recall problems complicating eyewitness accounts, the individual prejudices of witnesses may alter how they perceive events. After observing a crime, witnesses may remember events differently depending on factors such as race or gender. Which of the following statements about prejudice is FALSE?

A.   Prejudice can refer to either positive or negative attitudes and/or beliefs regarding certain people based on the group to which those people belong.

B.   Cognitive prejudice describes a set of characteristics believed to be true of all members of a specific group. It can refer to either an in-group or an out-group.

C.   Affective prejudice describes emotions directed toward members of a specific group.

D.   Conative prejudice describes the actual actions taken toward members of a specific group.

Conative prejudice describes the tendency towards action (what someone *thinks* he or she would do), but doesn't describe the actual action itself. Conative prejudice is still classified as an attitude. For example, someone may think that he or she wouldn't lend a pencil to a Whootonite (and therefore would have a conative prejudice), but he may actually lend the pencil to a Whootonite when put in the position to do so. Therefore, **answer choice (D)** is false and is the correct answer to the question. All other statements are true.

With that, you're finished with the passage. But there are two more discrete questions, the first of which is about mental processing.

Question 30

A boy sees a sticklike figure that was moving on the ground coil itself up and begin to make a rattling noise. Using these independent clues collectively, he deduces that the figure is a rattlesnake. This order of actions best illustrates:

    A.   Weber's law.
    B.   signal detection theory.
    C.   top-down processing.
    D.   parallel processing.

The question stem defines a psychological phenomenon and asks for its identity. The details are a boy taking small facts and piecing them together to create a bigger picture. The key word here is "collectively." The boy is using clues at the same time to make a determination. This would correctly match **answer choice (D)**, parallel processing, which is defined as using clues in tandem to make a deduction.

Choice (A) is incorrect because Weber's Law is based on thresholds people experience. Choice (B) is also incorrect because signal detection theory is based on perception varying due to any extreme or harsh nature in stimulus (for example, a loud noise distracts someone from perceiving other stimuli). Lastly, answer choice (C) is incorrect because top-down processing would be the opposite, as it deals with using a larger understanding to infer details. The situation given is much closer to bottom-up processing.

Now let's move on to the last question, which covers evolution.

Question 31

Which of the following biological explanations for the existence of altruism in humans, if true, would pose the greatest challenge to Neo-Darwinism?

    A.   Humans primarily help those to whom they are related and do so because they share genes with these individuals, which compensates for any survival or reproductive disadvantage incurred from the altruistic act.

B.   Humans usually engage in altruistic behavior when there are others around to see and do so because this confers a reproductive advantage: those who witness acts of altruism will be more inclined to mate with the altruistic individual.

    C.   Humans have developed a keen sense for recognizing individuals who take but never give back, these "cheaters" are ostracized by a group, which decreases both the chance of survival and of reproducing.

    D.   Human societies that contain many altruistic individuals are able to outcompete those societies that contain many selfish individuals, leading to the predominance of altruistic cultures.

This is a question that tests your understanding of a number of concepts in evolutionary biology and psychology. First, you must be familiar with the technical definition of altruism, which refers to any behavior that imposes a cost on the actor and grants a concomitant benefit to the recipient of that action.

Next, it is essential to recognize that Neo-Darwinism, also known as "the modern synthesis" of Darwinian evolution and Mendelian genetics, assumes that all selection takes place in the competition between different individuals' genes. If a heritable trait, such as the tendency to engage in altruistic behavior, decreases survival or reproductive fitness without providing some compensatory advantage, it will be selected against and eventually disappear from the population.

In **answer choice (D)**, we are given an account of "group selection," in which evolution is supposed to be acting at the level of human groups or larger societies. Neo-Darwinians reject group selection; they would argue that altruism could not arise in any of these cultures in the first place (without some other explanation), because the altruistic act benefits others at a cost to oneself, decreasing one's fitness.

Choice (A) is incorrect because it is a summary of the theory known as "kin selection" or "inclusive fitness." For example, a mother may sacrifice her life to protect her child, who will still contain half of her genes. Under this account, selection is taking place at the level of genes, as the modern synthesis requires.

Choice (B) is incorrect because it is a paraphrase of the "fitness indicator theory," in which a reproductive advantage is able to compensate for a disadvantage in survival. For instance, a peacock must devote much of its energy to developing its illustrious tail, and said tail makes it harder to flee from predators. Nevertheless, peahens prefer those males with the most beautiful plumage, and won't breed with those who lack such indications of fitness. If a peacock can survive with that ridiculous tail, then it must be pretty fit! While it pits sexual selection against natural selection, it is still operating at the level of individuals and their genes.

Finally, choice (C) is incorrect because it is an explanation for the existence of reciprocal altruism. Putting yourself at a disadvantage to benefit another person is not a problem if that person turns around and helps you out tomorrow. Overall, reciprocal relationships heighten the fitness of any who participate in them. The capacity to detect cheaters is then essential, because cheaters violate reciprocity, receiving benefits without imposing costs on themselves (putting the other members of their population at relative disadvantage). The presence of cheater detection will lead to selection for individuals who do their fair share and who are willing to help others now if it means help for them later.

Psychological, Social, and Biological Foundations of Behavior tests many of the concepts taught in undergraduate sociology and psychology, along with topics from various biology classes as well. It is a good idea to start studying these concepts now, and especially to get plenty of practice with the types of questions that will be in this section of the MCAT 2015. With steady practice, this new section of the MCAT 2015 can get you a great score!

CHAPTER 13

MCAT 2015 Practice Test

Thus far in this book, you have read a lot about the MCAT 2015. Ideally, you are very well versed and feel confident about the nature of the new exam at this point. Just think—you have not only learned about the evolution of the test, but you have also followed along as we worked through examples and strategies necessary to be successful on an exam that will first appear in the spring of 2015. However, reading about the test is really just the beginning. For true success on and preparedness for the new exam, practice is a must. In this chapter, it's the time to put your newly acquired skills into practice.

Given that the AAMC has only released a small subset of practice materials, it would be a little premature for any student to take a full-length practice test at this point. Nevertheless, taking a short-form version of MCAT 2015 may be just what the doctor ordered (pun intended). Such a test would allow you to put the knowledge and skills you learned in this book into practice, and that is perfectly appropriate at this point. Fortunately, we have created such a test for you and that's what we're going to do next.

Based on our examination of the AAMC's *Preview Guide for the MCAT2015 Exam*, as well as the analysis and contributions of our very own psychometrician, Kaplan has developed an MCAT 2015 practice test that represents one-third of the time and content of the full-length MCAT 2015. This practice test, as of the printing of this publication, is our best guess as to what MCAT 2015 will look like. Taking this practice test is meant to expose you to the new test's content and format, as well as give you the opportunity to try out the strategies and skills you learned in this book.

Just remember, this is only a short-form version of MCAT 2015. This means that it represents a small sample of the questions. Therefore, we want you to use it as such—a chance to be exposed to a subset of test questions in their natural testing environment. As you take the practice test, remember that while it is an exercise of the test-taking skills you have recently acquired, it is also a step forward in your journey toward wearing that white coat!

So take a deep breath, relax, reflect on what you now know and dive into this MCAT 2015 Practice Test. In the next chapter, we will discuss how to use your performance on the practice test to shape the next part of your journey.

All of the instructions you need for taking the MCAT 2015 Practice Test are at www.kaptest.com/mcat2015. That is our MCAT 2015 homepage, and the registration link for the test is there. When you are finished with the practice test, take some time to reflect on how it felt compared to tests you are used to taking. Then, we will tackle the next steps together in the chapters to come.

Good luck!

CHAPTER 14

Interpreting Your Practice Test Score

First and foremost, congratulations! You are now even closer to wearing a white coat. And the fact that you have already taken a practice test for the MCAT 2015 puts you so much further ahead of your peers.

Second, take a deep breath. The results of the practice test are not final. In other words, there is plenty of time to improve your scores as you continue to hone your test-taking skills and content knowledge.

And lastly, before we dive into a deeper analysis of the results, recognize that this was just a dry run, your first time incorporating the myriad of information you have amassed from this book.

So let's start out with the big question: **What do the results mean?**

This test is short-form for a very specific reason. Now is not the time to be taking a full-length MCAT 2015; in fact, that time will not come until a couple of months before you take the official exam. Often, students think that the best way to study for the MCAT, new or old, is to take multiple practice tests without changing anything about their test-taking behavior. What did Albert Einstein say? "Insanity is doing the same thing over and over again and expecting different results." Sound familiar? The last thing you want to be doing at this point is simply repeating your behavior, especially in the areas that you didn't have as much success in as you'd like. So let's analyze your results and see where you can change your patterns to achieve an even higher score the next time you look at MCAT 2015.

Did you use the strategies that you acquired in the worked examples of each of the section types? If the answer is yes, then you are on the right path. But chances are, you still didn't get everything correct. After all, mastering a test does not happen overnight. What you want to do now is reflect on the test you just took and use it as a study tool to launch the next steps in your preparation for MCAT 2015. Let's take a look how to understand your results.

USING THE KAPTEST.COM INTERFACE

If you go back to the online practice test on Kaptest.com, you should see a screen like this:

Test Sections	
Chemical and Physical Foundations of Biological Systems	Go
Critical Analysis and Reasoning Skills	Go
Biological and Biochemical Foundations of Living Systems	Go
Psychological Social and Biological Foundations of Behavior	Go

Your percent correct is an overall percentage correct from the test, all questions included.

You will see that each section has a "GO" button next to it. If you click on the GO button next to, say, the Chemical and Physical Foundations of Biological Systems section, you will see a detailed, question-by-question analysis of your results:

	Q#	Answer Selected	Correct Answer	Previous Answer	Seconds Used
✔	1	D	D		278
✔	2	A	A		65
✔	3	C	C		31
✔	4	C	C		13
✘	5	A	D		380
✔	6	A	A		161
✔	7	B	B		65
✘	8	A	B		38
✔	9	C	C		26
✔	10	B	B		18
✘	11	A	B		31
✔	12	B	B		66
✔	13	D	D		12
✘	14	C	A		15
✔	15	C	C		16
✘	16	C	A		11
✘	17	B	D		26
✔	18	A	A		9
✔	19	A	A		104
✘	20	B	C		43

Green check marks mean you got the question correct, and red "X"s mean you got the question wrong. You will also see that both your answer and the correct answer are displayed, as well as any previous answers you changed during the course of the test. But the real benefit of this analysis comes into play when you look at the amount of time you spent on each question; more on that later!

Now let's go one step further. If you click the GO button next to each question, you will be taken to a detailed explanation of that question and its answer choices.

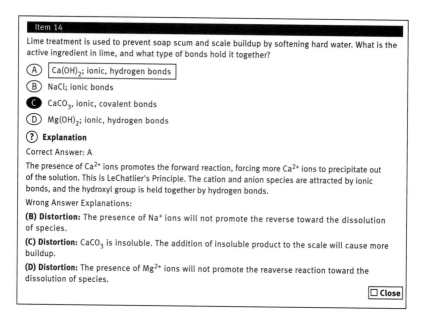

For this example, the question was answered incorrectly. The student's answer is still marked (C), but the correct answer is boxed in green. But, even better, the explanation for the logic of the question, as well as for why each wrong answer is incorrect, is also listed. You will want to use these explanations to understand the reasoning behind this specific question, but also to start to identify patterns in your performance.

So now that you know how to read the results, let's talk about what to do with them.

HOW TO REVIEW THE PRACTICE TEST

Start by going through the entire test—question by question, passage by passage—and reflect on your performance.

Timing

If you spent a lot of time and got a question wrong, we want you to ask yourself these questions: Was it worth it? Could I have spent the time getting another question or multiple questions correct? Why did I spend a lot of time? Often students will find that perfectionism drives them to invest a sizable chunk of time into a challenging question because they feel the need to finish a question once they've started it. Knowing when to give up on a question is a strategy—not a weakness! This may be true for heavy plug-and-chug questions that require a lot of math; even if you *know* that you could solve the math to get the correct answer, the amount of time it may take you to get to that answer might not be worth it. Note that it is normal—even expected—to have spent a lot of time on the first question of each passage, since that would have been time you were invested in actually *reading* the passage.

TEST DAY TIP

Knowing when to give up on a question is a strategy—not a weakness! It's not worth spending a ton of time on a single question, even if you know that you'll be able to get it right at the end of your work. Come back to this question after you've worked on the rest of the questions associated with that passage. If it's still going to take too long to work through the question at that point, "mark" it and come back at the end of the section.

How was your timing from passage to passage? Was there one passage that ended up weighing you down, forcing you to lose time you could be working on simpler passages? If so, look for clues that would have told you to skip this passage for the time being, and come back to it at the end of the section. On the contrary, what clues could indicate that a passage would be relatively quick to work through? While this differs somewhat from person to person, passages that are mostly visual (flowcharts, large tables of information, many graphs) will not require much time to read and map. Choosing passages that focus on topics you're already stronger in to "warm up" on at the beginning of the section can be a very effective way to speed you up on Test Day.

TEST DAY TIP

Choosing passages that focus on topics you're already strong in to warm up with at the beginning of the section can be a very effective way to speed you up on Test Day. Other criteria for choosing what order to do the passages in include: passage length, length of individual paragraphs, breakdown of visual information versus text, syntax, keywords, passage type, number of associated questions, amount of math involved in these questions, and so on. It's a skill to be able to size-up a passage in 3 to 5 seconds, but that should be your goal. That way, you spend only a couple minutes coming up with your plan of attack and then just execute it during the course of your MCAT.

Passages

For passages, take a look at your scratch paper and compare your passage map to the "ideal" passage map given in the explanations. A great exercise at this point is to go back and reread the passages and recreate the passage map a second time. You'll likely find that, now that you've had the opportunity to work through the questions, it's easier to map the passage quickly and effectively. This actually provides you with a lot of insight into how to critically read passages the next time around. Ask yourself some questions again: What information turned out to be important in this passage? What parts of the passage did they reference, or did I have to come back to, in order to answer a question? How do they hint that these details would be important—were there key words, visual emphasis (italics or quotation marks), or heavily opinionated words used in these sentences? By turning your pattern from "passive reading" (reading with equal emphasis on all parts of the passage, waiting for important information to come along) to "active reading" (being engaged with the passage to more easily spot this important text) to "critical reading" (anticipating where the author is going to go, assessing arguments in real time, and predicting what questions you'll see associated with the passage) you will be more successful with the passages.

TEST DAY TIP

The more you can anticipate where the author's going to go, the better. If the author sticks to what you expect, it'll be easier to absorb the important information and quickly create a passage map. If the author breaks from what you expected, that should be interesting to you—since it's certainly interesting to the test makers! By extension, that point would likely be tested in the questions. Essentially, the more you think like the author of the passage, the more you'll think like the test makers. And the more you think like the test makers, the more you'll answer questions like the test makers (correctly!).

Think about how you worked through that passage. Were you able to move quickly and get to the questions, or did you find yourself getting stuck in difficult wording or complicated sentences? The harder the passage, the less you want to struggle. Think of this like quicksand: What happens when you're stuck in quicksand and you struggle? You sink deeper. The same thing will happen with a killer passage. The more you try to understand every little detail, the more you're going to sink into the quicksand and lose the big picture.

MED SCHOOL INSIGHT

Why do you think MCAT passages tend to have way more information in them than you could memorize, let alone get tested on? The skills in working through a passage like this will translate to your work as a clinician during patient interviews. When a patient presents with a complicated history, you'll have to distinguish what information is helpful in making the diagnosis from what are just extraneous details. It will also be useful when you have to consolidate hundreds of pages of patient notes, nursing orders, and laboratory results down to a straightforward medical history.

Then step back from that one passage alone, and look at how you did on passages as a whole. Do you tend to do better on passages that are just providing information, or on ones that present an experiment and its conclusions? In Critical Analysis and Reasoning Skills, do you do better on passages in the humanities (art history, literature, musicology, philosophy, and so forth) or in the social sciences (cultural studies, economics, political science, anthropology, and so forth)?

Questions

For the questions, start to see if you can recognize patterns in the type of wrong answer choices you gravitated toward. There are many categories of wrong answer choices: distortions, faulty use of detail, and opposites, just to name a few. One recommendation we make to our students is to create charts called "Why I Missed It Sheets" to track your performance and help you identify patterns in areas you will want to work on.

Here is an example of a chart you can make for this question:

Section	Question Number	Content Area	Why I Missed It
Chem/Phys	#14	Ions, Le Châtelier's Principle	Distortion: misinterpreted solubility rules

As you go through this exam, this chart will get longer and longer, and will start to create clarity into the content areas you will want to go back to in your studies to ensure you have a very strong grasp on them.

For the science sections, stick to the format of this chart; for CARS, consider changing the "Content Area" column to be a "CARS skills" column (since no outside knowledge is necessary). For the last column ("Why I Missed It"), think deeply about what you choose to write. Your answer should never be that you made a "stupid mistake," or that "If it were the *real* MCAT, I would have gotten it!" These do not help you to learn from your mistakes, which—ultimately—is the entire purpose of practice materials like this practice test. While your reasons for why you missed questions may include a number of content points that you simply need to fill in, be on the lookout for what *your* specific test-taking errors are. Do you frequently misread questions, missing a "NOT," "EXCEPT," "FALSE," or "LEAST"? Do you have difficulty manipulating equations and data sets in order to reach the correct answer? Do you figure out the correct answer, only to accidentally hit the wrong answer choice before submitting the section? Only by identifying the mistakes that you make can you address these mistakes and turn them into points on Test Day.

MED SCHOOL INSIGHT

In many hospitals, it is routine for a team involved in a code (emergency resuscitation of a patient on the floors) to come back at a later date and recreate the entire scenario, paying attention to what went well and what could have been improved. There is some evidence that this improves patient outcomes in the long run, mainly by improving communications between physicians, nurses, and support staff, and generally increasing the amount of experience the whole team has with code situations. **Think of your review of your MCAT as your chance to rerun a code: What went well? What could have been improved? Identify what's keeping you from the score you deserve on Test Day and fix it.**

As previously mentioned, assess how you did on CARS questions by focusing on the CARS skills covered in Chapter 11. Often, students find that they spend an exorbitant amount of time on Comprehension questions, even though they consider them the easiest to answer. This is especially true for detail-oriented questions, or *scattered* detail-oriented questions (ones that include Roman numerals or "NOT" in them). This should not be surprising, since these questions require you to go back to the passage and find not one, but four separate pieces of information to answer the question. On the other hand, students often find that they have many missed answers with Reasoning Beyond the Text questions (both Application and Incorporation subtypes). These require you to apply new information into the passage, or apply information from the passage to a new scenario. Often, this form of lateral thinking is somewhat new to MCAT students; with practice on quality resources, you'll quickly learn how to answer these questions with ease.

CHAPTER LINK

Check out Chapter 11 for a breakdown of the Scientific Inquiry and Reasoning Skills (tested in the science sections), as well as the CARS skills tested on MCAT 2015.

Next Steps

Once you have gone through the entire practice test, take a break (even for a day or two), and then go back to your chart and start thinking about the content areas on which you need to focus. Content is the foundation of MCAT 2015. The test is written in the language of science. The reward of a high score, however, comes from being able to apply the content that you know to an unfamiliar context—*that's* how you get more points. So before you do any more practice, you will want to consider the content areas you did not perform well on and ask yourself whether it is content that you have seen before and need to either relearn or refresh yourself on, or if it is content that is completely new to you.

For the content that you need a refresher on (courses you took in college or perhaps received Advanced Placement credit for), there are plenty of resources you could go to. And even for the content that is foreign to you, there are still plenty of resources to check out. In fact, Chapters 9 and 10 lay out strategies for class scheduling and appropriate resources to use if you haven't taken a particular class already. In a weird way, content knowledge is free. It's the "easy" step on the way to mastering MCAT 2015. What you will want and need to do at this point is start to fill in your content knowledge gaps. This might mean taking a course in some subject areas that you haven't yet taken. Or it might mean finding some resources online.

CHAPTER LINK

Chapters 9 focuses on creating a course schedule based on the prerequisites for MCAT 2015. Chapter 10 lists resources for studying material for classes which you may not have taken.

But as we said before, the real win on the MCAT comes with the *application* of that content. So this is why you will want to shift your focus back to the test itself. Go back into the test armed with the content that you now have learned, and revisit all of the questions: the ones you missed, the ones you guessed, and even the ones you got right. Practice the application of the content in the same way we did in the worked examples in chapter 12.

The practice test tests you just like the actual MCAT 2015—requiring both content and critical thinking at the same time. But it's worth noting as you start your preparation for this exam that you will at first want to separate the two exercises. You will want to master the content first—lay the proper foundation—and then go after the application of that content. So in many ways, you dove in feet first by taking the practice test. But it's a good thing that you did, because it's an invaluable exercise to really give you the full perspective of the exam.

These practice test scores do not tell you how you will perform on MCAT 2015 on Test Day. They *do* tell you what you need to work on in order to set yourself up for the greatest success when you take MCAT 2015. These practice test results are meant to give you a starting point. As we alluded to before, this is just the beginning of your journey with MCAT 2015. Use these results to shape the next steps of your MCAT preparation. And, most importantly, as you tackle new questions in your practice, apply the skills and lessons learned so that you become a stronger and stronger test taker!

CHAPTER 15

A Few Final Thoughts

Now that you have analyzed your performance on the practice test, it's time to start considering which version of the test you will take if you have the choice. For those of you who are still in the early part of your premedical education, the choice is pretty clear: you more than likely will have to take MCAT 2015. But you might also be at the fork in the road where you really have the option to take either version.

Not that you want to take yet another test to assess your decision, but there is an opportunity to take a practice test of the current MCAT on our website (kaplanmcat.com/practice). You might find it helpful to see how much of the current test is still going to be on MCAT 2015, and since you have taken the practice test and read this book, you know what areas are going to be added.

MCAT 2015 is going to be longer. It is going to require more content knowledge. And it is going to be a more exhausting day because of these two elements. Studying for MCAT 2015 is also going to be more time-consuming. But you definitely don't want to rush into taking the MCAT now just to take a shorter test!

So ask yourself if you have the time to take the prerequisite courses necessary for MCAT 2015. Which test will make you stand out the best as an applicant? Are you better at the application of the physical and biological sciences in the new or old context of the exam? Are biochemistry, psychology, and sociology strong suits of yours, or can they be? Regardless of which version you may take, know that medical schools are placing greater value on the skills and knowledge the new content areas bring. After all, they were the impetus for this test change, because they want students to be better prepared for success in medical school and in a career in medicine.

The short version of all of this is that if you have the opportunity, the choice of which version of the MCAT to take is ultimately going to be yours. You definitely don't want to rush your premedical requirements just to take the current MCAT, but at the same time, you must consider if you will have the time to complete the prerequisites for MCAT 2015.

Whatever you decide, you will make the best choice for yourself. This book has given you that jump start into getting ready for MCAT 2015, but the work is only beginning. We hope that you take the lessons learned here to propel yourself closer to that white coat!